Copyright © 2023 All rights reserved.
No part of these lessons or website may be reproduced
without the author's permission.

Scriptures taken from the Holy Bible, New International Version®, NIV®. Copyright © 1973, 1978, 1984, 2011 by Biblica, Inc.™ Used by permission of Zondervan. All rights reserved worldwide. www.zondervan.com The "NIV" and "New International Version" are trademarks registered in the United States Patent and Trademark Office by Biblica, Inc.™

GOD of the WORD
BIBLE STUDY

Promised Land I

STUDY OF JOSHUA - 1 SAMUEL 12

Table of Contents

6	A Letter on Salvation
9	Foreword by Mark M. Yarbrough
10	About the Author and Preface
13	Weekly Structure
14	Instructions
16	Story of the Bible

LEADERS

123	Leader's Manual
142	Lesson Answers

EXTRA RESOURCES

41	Joshua's Campaigns Map
53	Tribal Division of Canaan

19	**Introduction**
23	**Lesson 1: Preparation for Conquest** Joshua 1:1-5:12
33	**Lesson 2: The Campaigns** Joshua 5:13-12:24
45	**Lesson 3: Division of the Land** Joshua 13-24
57	**Lesson 4: Causes of Israel's Decline, Deborah, Gideon** Judges 1-9
67	**Lesson 5: Jephthah, Samson, Consequences of Decline** Judges 10-21
77	**Lesson 6: Naomi's Story** Ruth 1-4
87	**Lesson 7: Samuel's Birth and Call** 1 Samuel 1-3
97	**Lesson 8: The Exile of the Ark and Samuel's Leadership** 1 Samuel 4-7
107	**Lesson 9: Monarchy: Saul and Samuel** 1 Samuel 8-12
117	**Lesson 10: Looking it Over** Joshua-1 Samuel 12

A Letter on Salvation

I am writing to you because of your desire to be in heaven one day and the confusion of so many about the nature of Christian faith. It is tragic when people live with no hope, but it is equally tragic for people to live with false hope. The truth is that many who claim to be Christians are either uninformed or misinformed about the nature of Biblical faith. "Christians" talk very little about sin these days, which contributes greatly to the problem. This is especially disconcerting since the Bible says so much about it. In fact, without personal conviction of guilt for one's sin, the Christian message is meaningless. The gospel ("good news") of the Bible is only good news to those who know that they need saving.

The preaching of Jesus and Paul starts in much the same way that the Bible starts, with facts concerning sin in the world and the universal guilt of human beings. Each of us is guilty because we have inherited a sin nature from our first father, Adam, and also because we have each personally sinned against God. One only has to consider the Ten Commandments to see how short we all fall of His holy standard. Is there one of us who has not stolen something (have you never once stolen someone's reputation with a careless, slanderous word)? Is there one of us who has not secretly loved (worshipped) anyone or anything in the way that only the Creator deserves? Is there anyone who has never dishonored his or her parents, even privately? Who has never once lied, never even stretched the truth just a little? The apostle Paul stated it clearly: "There is no one righteous, not even one... for all have sinned and fall short of the glory of God" (Romans 3:10, 23). Furthermore, the penalty for sin is permanent, spiritual death, which is separation from God throughout eternity [Romans 6:23]. According to the Bible, sin is our main problem. Yet too often, the focus of the Christian message as we hear today has little, if anything, to do with sin.

A second point of confusion about Christianity revolves around the solution to our "sin problem." Many people who realize their sin nature hope to please God and earn their way to heaven on their own merit. The trouble is that the Bible does not teach salvation by works. In fact, it indicates that nothing we do will ever enable us to reach God (Romans 3:9-18). He is too holy and we are too sinful. The gap is too wide for any person to bridge by his or her own good works. In Romans 1:17, the apostle Paul quotes from the Old Testament book of Habakkuk: "For in the gospel a righteousness from God is revealed, a righteousness that is by faith from first to last, just as it is written, 'The righteous will live by faith.'" What was Paul's point? He quoted from the Old Testament because in those times, God's people lived under an obligation to the Law. Nevertheless, Paul points out that even in that day, those whom God deemed "righteous" were those who lived by faith. In other words, the Law was never intended to save anyone, because none could keep it perfectly. God knew of our inability long before He gave the Law. According to Paul, the Law serves to magnify our awareness of the unfathomable gap between God and us: "No one will be declared righteous in His sight by observing the law; rather, through the law we become conscious of sin" (Romans 3:20). The purpose of the Law is to show us just how far we fall short of God's standard.

With these things in mind, the gospel (good news) makes sense: God bridged the gap for us, providing a righteousness apart from the Law through Jesus Christ and our faith in Him (Romans 3:21-22). Jesus not only died to pay the death penalty we owe to God for our sin, He also lived the perfect life that none of us could have lived. If we put our faith in Christ, God is graciously willing to accept Jesus' death in substitute of our own and credit us with Jesus' righteousness. Thus, "the righteous will live by faith" (Romans 1:17) and "a man is justified by faith apart from observing the law" (Romans 3:28). We contribute nothing to our salvation. Jesus has done everything, and our only hope is faith in Him.

Why then does the Bible say so much about obedience and good works? First, the Bible insists that God's people cannot live blessed lives if they are not obedient to God's commands (Luke 11:28). It also says that obedience and good works will be the basis of each believer's heavenly rewards (2 Corinthians 5:10, Colossians 3:24, Revelation 22:12). Most importantly, it says that good works are an essential evidence of salvation. Those who are "in Christ" and going to Heaven will naturally want to please God (James 1-5, 1 John 2:3). Conversely, anyone who isn't eager to obey God probably isn't saved.

Tragically, many people who think they will go to heaven, even those who call themselves "Christians," will not, for two reasons. Too often, people believe their good works will balance out the debt they owe God. Many also take "faith in Christ" too lightly, as though it is merely an easy, comfortable road to happiness, rather than as a challenging but rewarding road to holiness. But doesn't the Bible say that God has a wonderful plan for our lives? Yes, it does. It says that God's wonderful plan is to make us more like Christ (Romans 8:28-29). The Christian life is a rich life (John 10:10), but it is not a pain-free life (John 16:33). We should not assume that being a Christian is an easy thing, requiring only a quick prayer or intellectual assent to Christ's person and work. Trusting Christ to save us involves a commitment of our lives into His service and a commitment to suffering for the sake of His reputation and the hardship in promoting His purposes. True, saving faith involves shifting our loyalty from self-interests to God's interests. The Christian's joy is not the result of a trouble-free life. Christian joy comes from the assurance that after death we are guaranteed an eternal, heavenly home!

If you have never had this assurance before or never understood the nature of true, saving faith, today can be the day of your salvation. Will you "declare with your mouth, 'Jesus is Lord,' and believe in your heart that God raised Him from the dead" with this understanding of the implications? If so, "you will be saved" (Romans 10:9).

With Christ's love for you,

D. A. Hammond

> **because, if you confess with your mouth that Jesus is Lord and believe in your heart that God raised him from the dead, you will be saved.**
>
> **ROMANS 10:9**

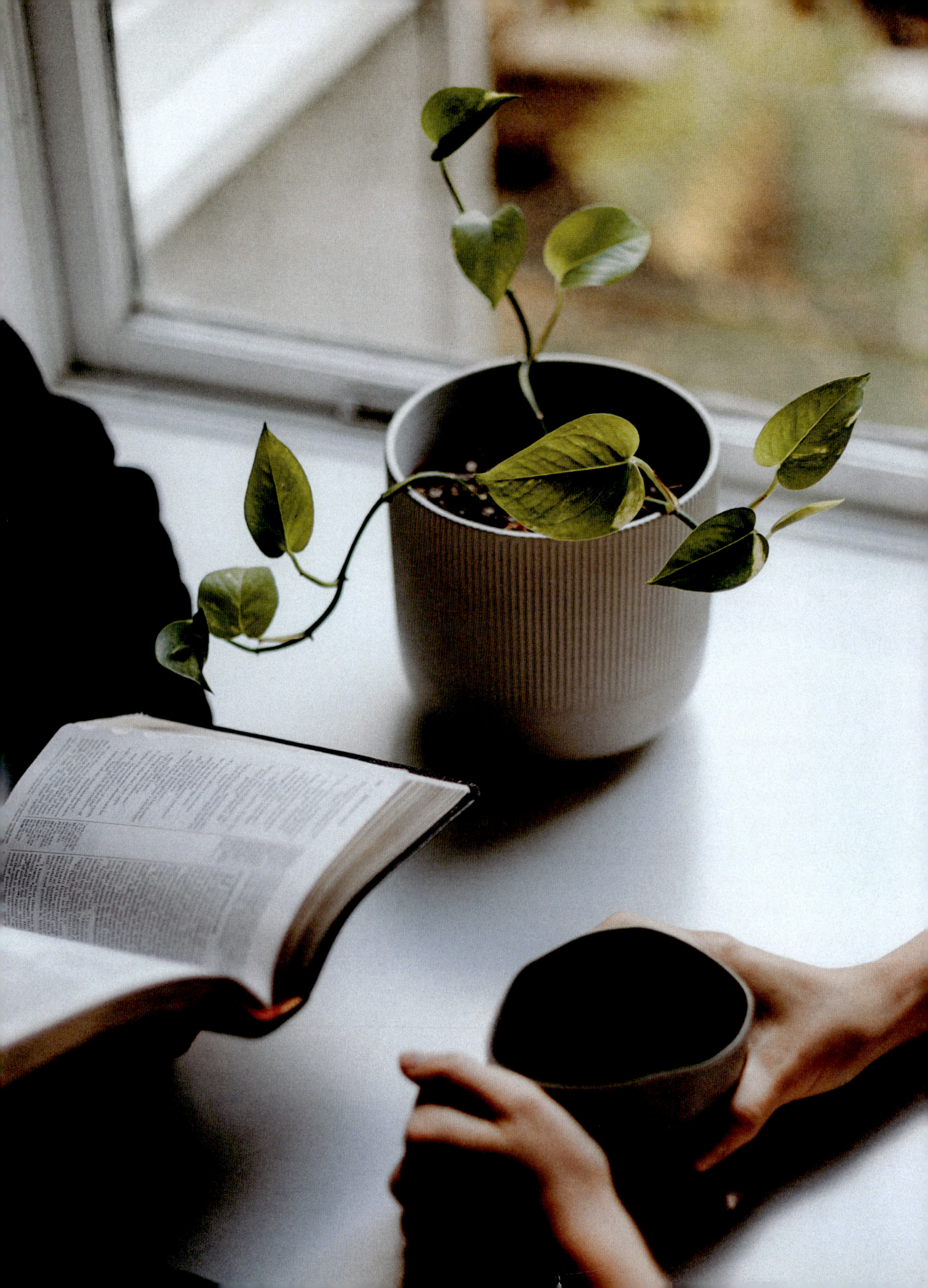

Foreword

We live in a time when people burn their hands not on campfires but on microwavable dinners. Simply put: our culture is in a hurry. As impatience abounds, people often prefer quick and immediate results over the fruits of hard work. This expedited method predictably does not work when it comes to personal relationships. Without spending quality time with someone, it is unrealistic to expect to know someone fully.

Our relationship with God follows a similar path. We must marinate in His Word to foster a healthy relationship with Him. We must go beyond the occasional reading of Christian posts and listening to our favorite pastors, as helpful as both may be. While these nuggets can undoubtedly encourage us, their brevity alone cannot fully illuminate the triune God of the Scripture. As a rule of thumb, the better you want to get to know someone, the more time you will need to spend with them.

As the president of Dallas Theological Seminary, I get the pleasure of promoting our long-standing mission of glorifying God by equipping godly servant-leaders for the proclamation of His Word and the building up of the body of Christ worldwide. We uphold this mission through six core values, the first of which is "Trust in God's Word." Trusting God requires knowing Him and knowing Him comes through spending time with Him. Not only can we experience the love of God through His creation, but also through Spirit-led in-depth studies of God's Word. You are holding in your hand that type of series.

The GOD of the WORD Bible Studies counteract our culture's current default of quick-fix mentality and single-verse theology. This study moves you from simply wearing a Christian t-shirt to understanding the text from whence it came. It invites learners into a beautiful understanding of the overarching story of the Bible. It is difficult to know God's Word if you do not study it and it is difficult to study it if you do not have solid study habits. These studies help solve this chain of challenges by offering guidance and direction for believers to sit and soak in Scripture.

Debbi Hammond invites new and experienced Bible students into a deep and systematic study of Holy Scripture. She brings her long history of teaching and leading inductive Bible studies to one's time with God. Debbi's interactive approach motivates students to dive daily into personal study with the help of a learning community and instructive videos. Through this series, she forms a thoughtful approach that will undoubtedly benefit those who join her on the journey of encountering God each day.

Debbi also desires to show followers of Jesus Christ how the books of the Bible fit together. I love that! Her goal is to encourage participants to experience firsthand the transforming power of God's Word and come to know it as living, active, practical, and applicable to everyday life. Her main textbook for the spiritual life is the Bible, and her studies seek to build biblical literacy in Christians and to build up the body of Christ around the world. The Lord gave us the Scripture to show how much He truly cares for us. May we all strive to study the most extraordinary love letter ever told, and in doing so, fall in love with its author all over again. Blessing to you as you embark upon this journey.

Mark M. Yarbrough, Ph.D.
President
Professor of Bible Exposition
Dallas Theological Seminary

About the Study

GOD of the WORD is a series of eight Bible studies that takes you through the Bible from beginning to end. The systematic approach highlights the overall story of the Bible, encourages application to everyday life, and is helpful to anyone, whether they have never opened a Bible or have studied it for many years. The GOTW format encourages students to dig into Bible passages for themselves before reading commentary or hearing teaching on it. This is accomplished through a three-step process, which begins with personal Bible reading and the answering of fifteen weekly questions. The second step is small group discussion. Finally, participants watch a summarizing video. This start-on-your-own approach allows an understanding of the passages to develop progressively, an ideal way to learn, and deepens personal conviction that God's word is indeed living and active.

About the Author

Debbi Hammond is a longtime student of the Bible and Bible study methods. For ten years, she was involved with an international Bible study organization, ultimately lecturing on the Bible and training leaders weekly in Christian leadership principles. In 2005, Debbi left that position and moved from the southwestern United States to upstate New York, where her husband Jim assumed leadership of Gospel Volunteers, Inc. and CAMP-of-the-WOODS. Her work on GOD of the WORD began in 2008 and continues to the present. Debbi trains individuals in and outside the United States who use her curriculum and also serves in a variety of hosting and teaching roles at CAMP-of-the-WOODS. She is the daughter of Dr. and Mrs. David Denyer and has been married to Jim since 1981. She and Jim have four children and a growing number of grandchildren.

Preface

God's Promise
People often ask me how GOD of the WORD came to be. I suppose it really began in 1999 when local church leaders started telling me that I belonged in a teaching ministry. No opportunity for me to act on that initially presented itself, but four years later, one with a good bit of responsibility finally came. Although it seemed successful, it was short-lived, due to a cross-country move and a family crisis that required my full attention on the homefront. For several long years, I prayed and wondered, continuing to believe that God's call to teach had been unmistakable. Nevertheless, for the time being, I had to turn down every opportunity. During those now precious years of waiting, the words of Ephesians 3:20 repeatedly came to me like a promise - God does "immeasurably more than we ask or imagine." I certainly couldn't imagine how my situation would resolve, but regardless, I took Him at His word.

God's Invitation
God's surprises began with an invitation and what felt like a risk. Although our family crisis was still ongoing, my dear, supportive husband and I agreed that the time seemed right for me to test the waters. On a Thursday morning in 2008, I met with a group of women whom I did not know but who were eager to study the Bible. The only decisions I made in advance were that the Bible would be our sole text and that we would start where the Bible starts, in Genesis. A year later, the group numbered in the fifties. A woman asked, "Are we studying through the Bible?" The thought appealed to me. Then, the pastor of another attendee asked to use my curriculum. "What curriculum?" I thought. All I had at the time were my scratched-out notes. I knew the time had come for me to act as though God indeed wanted to do more than I could imagine.

God at Work
I have often thought that no one could have been more surprised by what God did than me. Within four years, He enabled me to develop a full Bible curriculum which was used both in and out of the United States. Then in 2012, an important Chinese house church leader requested that the eight studies be translated into Chinese. The result was an intensive four-year editing and revision process, culminating in widespread distribution in mainland China. God certainly does immeasurably more than we ask or imagine. Now, I am inviting you to become part of what God is doing. My prayer is that each person who uses this tool will better know and love *the God* of the word. He never ceases to amaze. To this day, His surprises have continued. To Him alone be the glory!

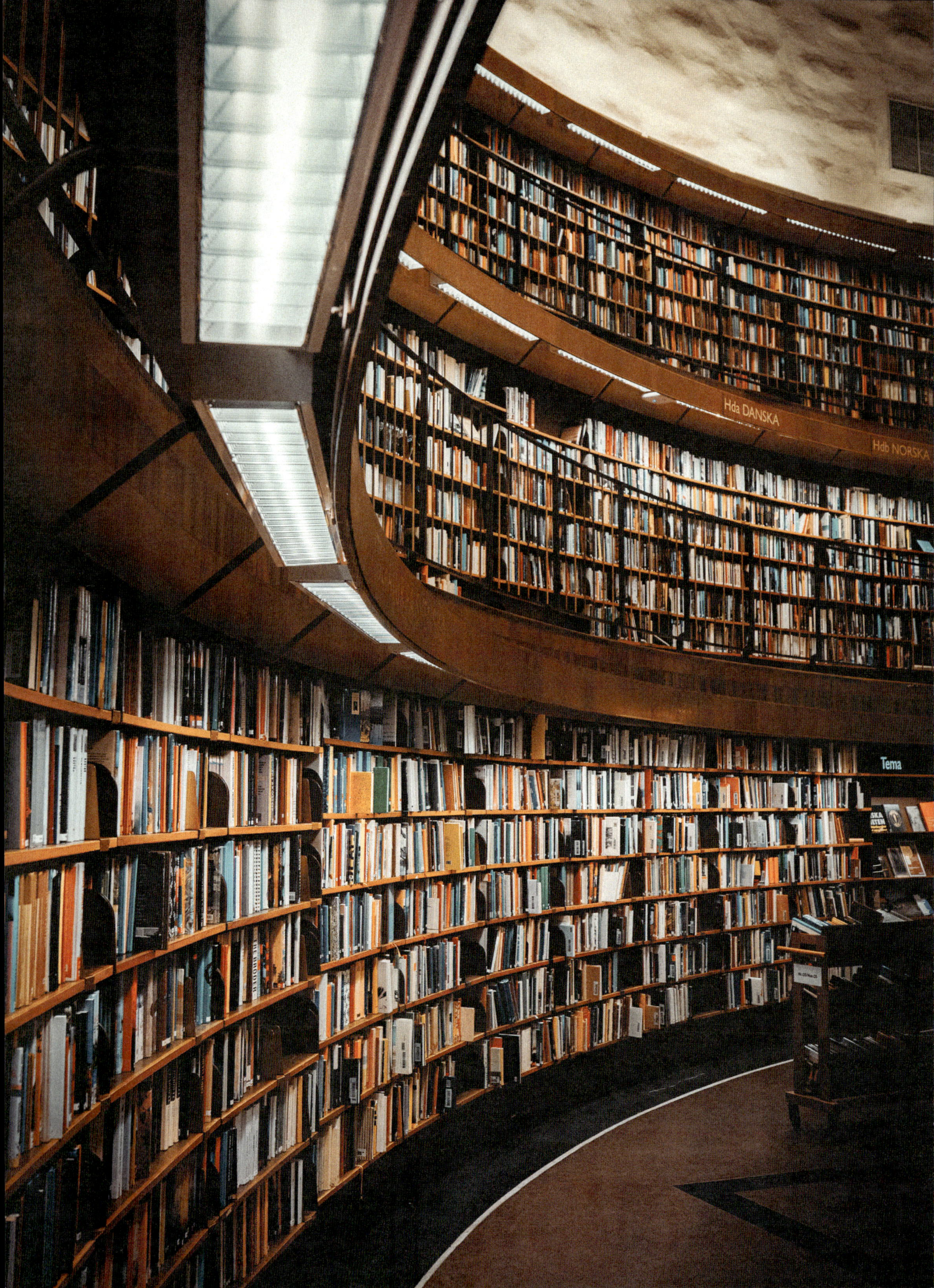
Hda DANSKA
Hdb NORSKA
Tema

Weekly Structure

INITIAL SMALL GROUP GATHERING

TIME:

_____   ▸ Meet and Greet
_____   ▸ Review Weekly Format below and Instructions (p. 14)
_____   ▸ Watch the Intro Video (roughly 35 minutes, p. 20)

FORMAT FOR YOUR GROUP

TIME:

_____   ▸ Arrival (and optional fellowship time)
_____   ▸ Discussion Period (40 min. recommended)
_____   ▸ Prayer Requests given and prayed over (roughly 15 min.)
_____   ▸ Break (optional)
_____   ▸ Closing Summary/Lesson Passage Video (roughly 35 min.)

GROW IN YOUR KNOWLEDGE OF GOD'S WORD

✓ Do your lesson faithfully
✓ Attend even when it is inconvenient
   (A very real enemy would like to deter you!)
✓ Determine in advance to persevere
   (Our format is deliberately different. It has been systematically developed and tested to support your group's success.)

✻ **For Individual Users:** The preferred three-step method of study involves small group discussion. For those who decide to use the workbook independently, please begin by watching the introductory video. Then, move on to Lesson 1, completing the weekly questions *before* watching each accompanying video.

Instructions

STEP 1

---PERSONAL READING & QUESTIONS---

🙏 PRAY BEFORE YOU START

Ask the Lord to reveal and forgive any sin in your life, to fill you anew, and to be your teacher. Recognize this is God's word to YOU, and it is LIVING!

📖 READ THE SCRIPTURE PASSAGE

Unless otherwise noted, the questions on each page refer to the passage(s) listed as readings at the top of each page. The primary Bible translation used in developing this study was the NIV, but you may use the translation of your choice.

✏ ANSWER QUESTIONS WITHOUT CONSULTING COMMENTARIES

A particular challenge of the GOD of the WORD study is to learn the joy of self-discovery guided by the Holy Spirit. It is always tempting and easier to look at what someone else has discovered rather than to think, study, and pray on your own. While commentaries and Study Bible notes are great enhancements to personal study, we ask that you wait until after your group meets to consult them. This may be a new approach to Bible study for some, but it is our conviction that you will ultimately find this practice to be more rewarding.

STEP 2

---SMALL GROUP DISCUSSION---

📝 HAVE LESSON COMPLETED

Please try to come prepared with your lesson completed. If you haven't had time to complete it, come anyway! Please give those who have done their lessons the courtesy of allowing them to do most of the talking.

🗣 ENCOURAGE GROUP PARTICIPATION

Talkative folks, please encourage quieter ones that their sharing is equally valuable by allowing them time to talk. Please don't let your feelings be hurt if your discussion leader must cut you off in order to give an opportunity to talk to those who are slower to share their answers. Be conscious that we are all at different levels of Bible knowledge.

❓ HOLD UNRELATED QUESTIONS

Ideally, you will participate in a group discussion that discusses all fifteen questions. Please enjoy hearty discussion without becoming frustrated if a thought and question that came to your mind in your personal study isn't explored. It will likely take all of the allotted discussion time just to cover the fifteen questions in the lesson. Your leader will help the group move through the lesson so that all of the questions will be discussed to some extent each week. You may find the extra information you are seeking in step three.

🤲 MAINTAIN SAFE SHARING ZONE

In order to foster an environment where group members feel comfortable talking honestly about their lives, please keep the things that are shared in the discussion confidential. Also, avoid offering advice. Most of us appreciate a "safe space" to confess our struggles without being told how to handle them.

🙏 PRAYER TIME

Your leader may devote a portion of your weekly meeting to prayer. Since those in your discussion group want to get to know you better during the study, it is recommended that prayer requests be limited to those asked for oneself. This is in no way intended to imply that prayer requests for others are less important or unworthy of group prayer. You are likely to want your prayer requests kept confidential, so please give others that same courtesy. Leaders are urged to make the giving of prayer requests or praying aloud in the group voluntary.

STEP 3
WATCH VIDEO

WATCH THE VIDEO

▶ After the discussion period, please watch the video. It summarizes and expands on the passage in your lesson. You will find the QR code leading to each video and an outline for note-taking immediately following your study and discussion questions in the workbook.

> * *If you plan on using a device other than your phone to watch the video, still scan the code. This will enable you to copy the link, paste it in an email to yourself, and then open the email on your computer. If you are projecting the video to watch in a group setting, open your email on the computer that is set up to the projector. Click the link and you're all set!*

LEADER'S NOTE

These instructions are GOD of the WORD distinctives. It's important to emphasize the benefit of them to your group. Be sure to ask, "Are we all in agreement?" after reading through the instructions to ensure everyone is committed to the study format.

STORY OF THE BIBLE

1. BEGINNINGS
- Creation
- The Fall
- The Flood
- Tower of Babel

2. PATRIARCHS
- Abraham
- Isaac
- Jacob
- Joseph

3. EXODUS
- Egypt
- Sinai
- Wilderness
- Border of Canaan

4. PROMISED LAND I
- The Land
- The Judges
- The Godly Remnant
- The First King

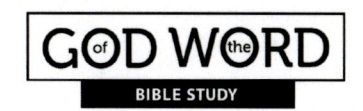

5. PROMISED LAND II

- United Kingdom
- Divided Kingdom
- Exile
- Resettlement

7. ACTS I

- Jerusalem
- Judea & Samaria
- The Uttermost Parts of the World

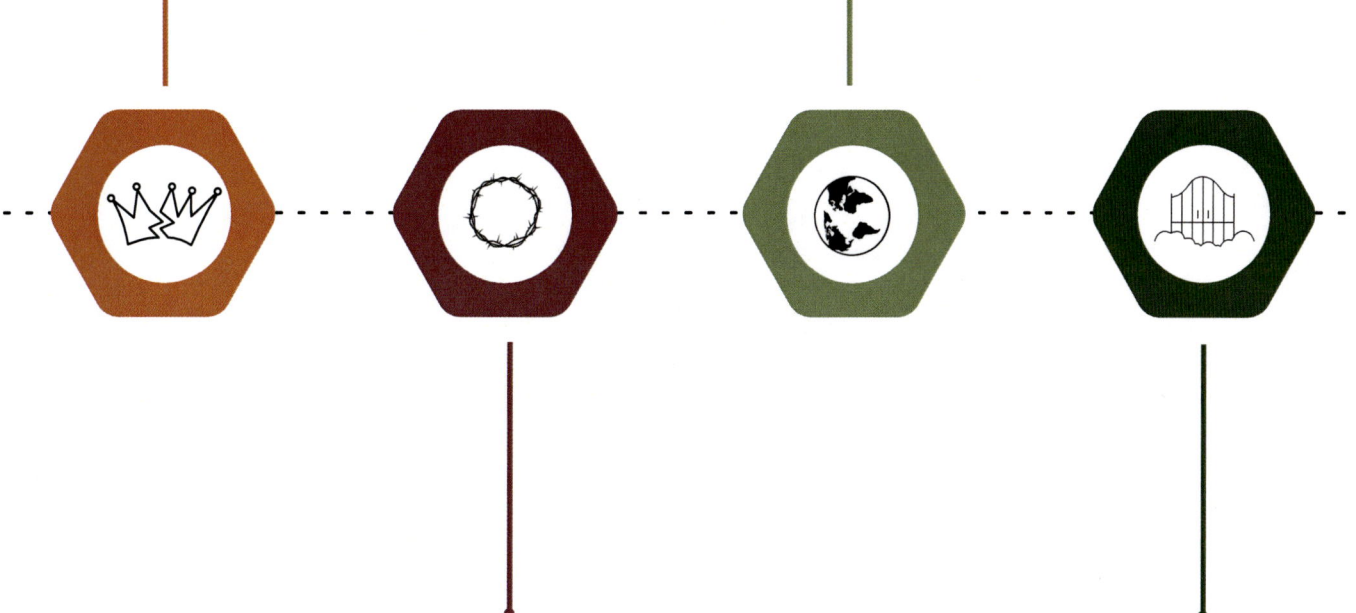

6. GOSPELS

- Messiah's Birth
- Messiah's Public Ministry
- Messiah's Training of the Disciples
- Messiah's Death & Triumph

8. ACTS II

- Paul's Imprisonment & Last Letters
- The Church in the Mid-to-Late First Century
- Revelation & Jesus' Return

Introduction

Introduction to *Promised Land I*

The Introductory Week has no lesson questions. This week you will review the weekly format with your group, as per the Weekly Structure on page 13. Then, watch the Introduction video on page 20.

The Land   **The Judges**   **The Godly Remnant**   **The First King**

"God offers His children **abundant life.**"

During your first meeting, point your phone camera here to view the Introductory Video.

Introduction to *Promised Land I*

Please use the QR code on the left-hand page to watch the Introductory Video before beginning Lesson 1 of the study.

I. Background to *Promised Land I*

Principle: We experience abundant life to the degree that we _____ _____ _____ _____ over us.

II. Overview of *Promised Land I*

Principle: Submission to God's authority begins with _____ _____ _____.

Lesson One

Preparation for Conquest

Joshua 1:1-5:12

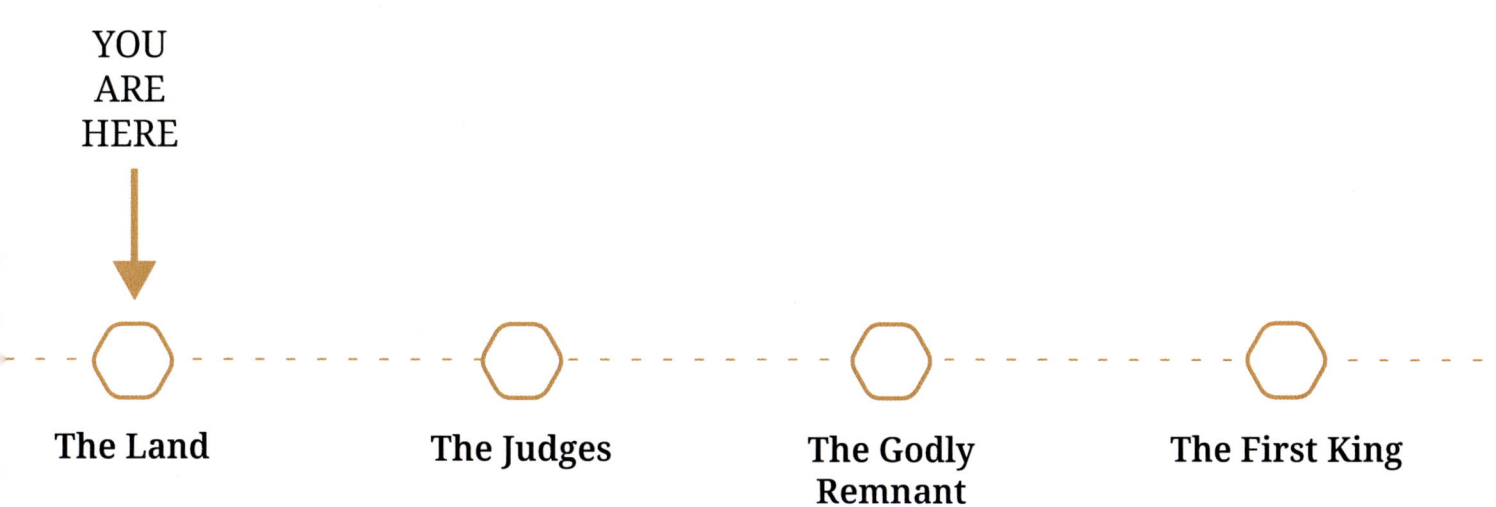

YOU ARE HERE ↓

○ The Land — ○ The Judges — ○ The Godly Remnant — ○ The First King

Day 1

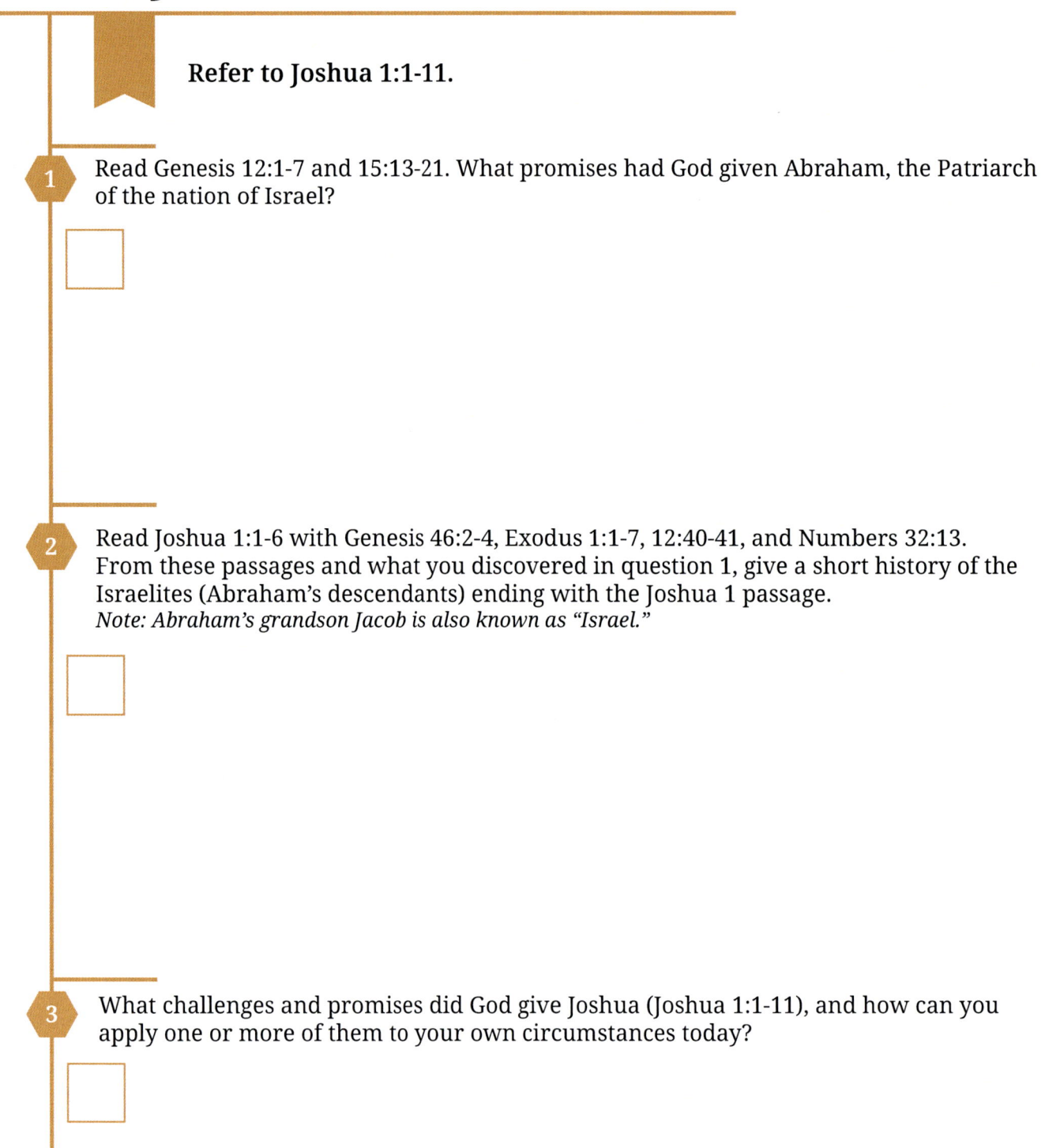

Refer to Joshua 1:1-11.

1. Read Genesis 12:1-7 and 15:13-21. What promises had God given Abraham, the Patriarch of the nation of Israel?

2. Read Joshua 1:1-6 with Genesis 46:2-4, Exodus 1:1-7, 12:40-41, and Numbers 32:13. From these passages and what you discovered in question 1, give a short history of the Israelites (Abraham's descendants) ending with the Joshua 1 passage.
Note: Abraham's grandson Jacob is also known as "Israel."

3. What challenges and promises did God give Joshua (Joshua 1:1-11), and how can you apply one or more of them to your own circumstances today?

Day 2

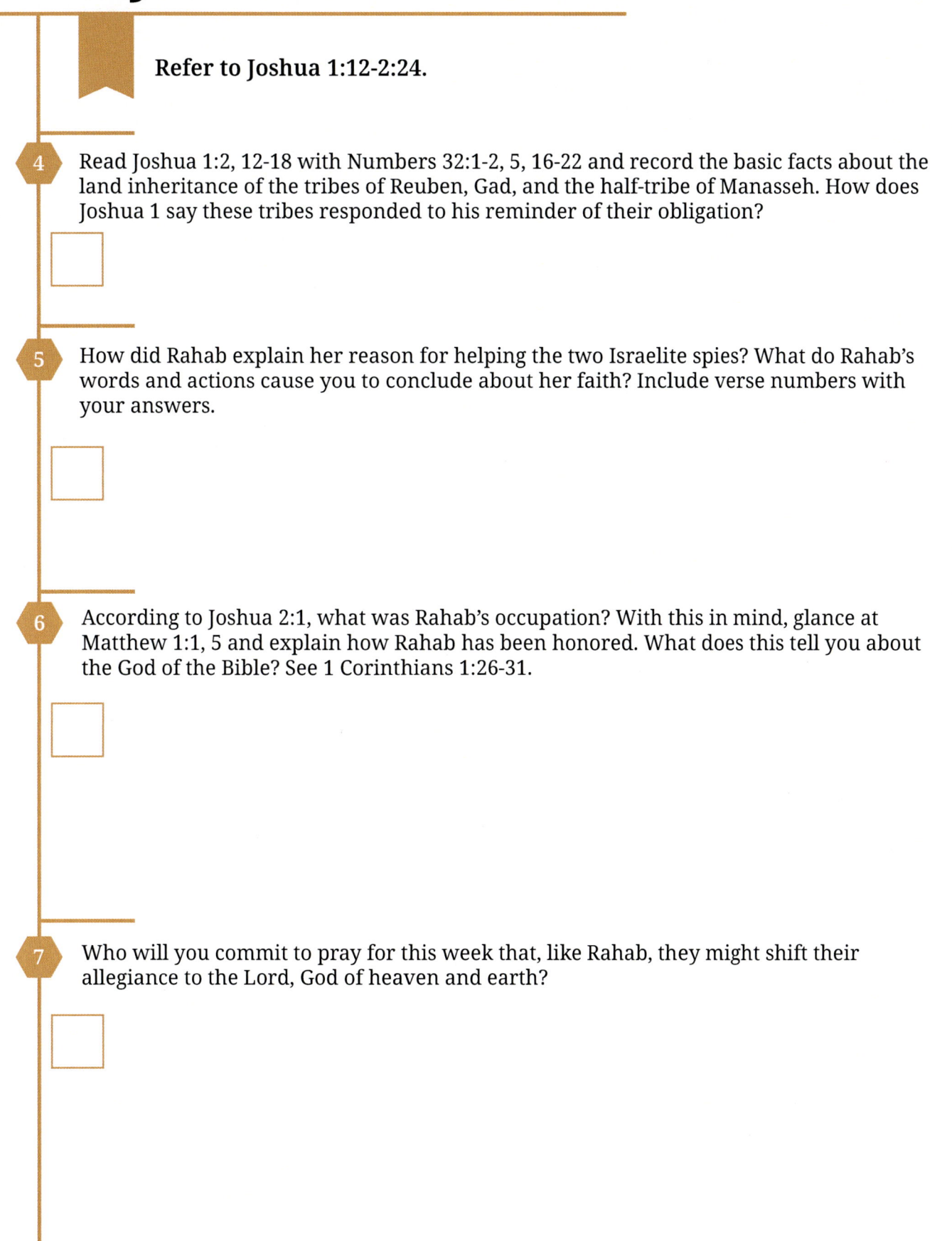

Refer to Joshua 1:12-2:24.

4 Read Joshua 1:2, 12-18 with Numbers 32:1-2, 5, 16-22 and record the basic facts about the land inheritance of the tribes of Reuben, Gad, and the half-tribe of Manasseh. How does Joshua 1 say these tribes responded to his reminder of their obligation?

5 How did Rahab explain her reason for helping the two Israelite spies? What do Rahab's words and actions cause you to conclude about her faith? Include verse numbers with your answers.

6 According to Joshua 2:1, what was Rahab's occupation? With this in mind, glance at Matthew 1:1, 5 and explain how Rahab has been honored. What does this tell you about the God of the Bible? See 1 Corinthians 1:26-31.

7 Who will you commit to pray for this week that, like Rahab, they might shift their allegiance to the Lord, God of heaven and earth?

Day 3

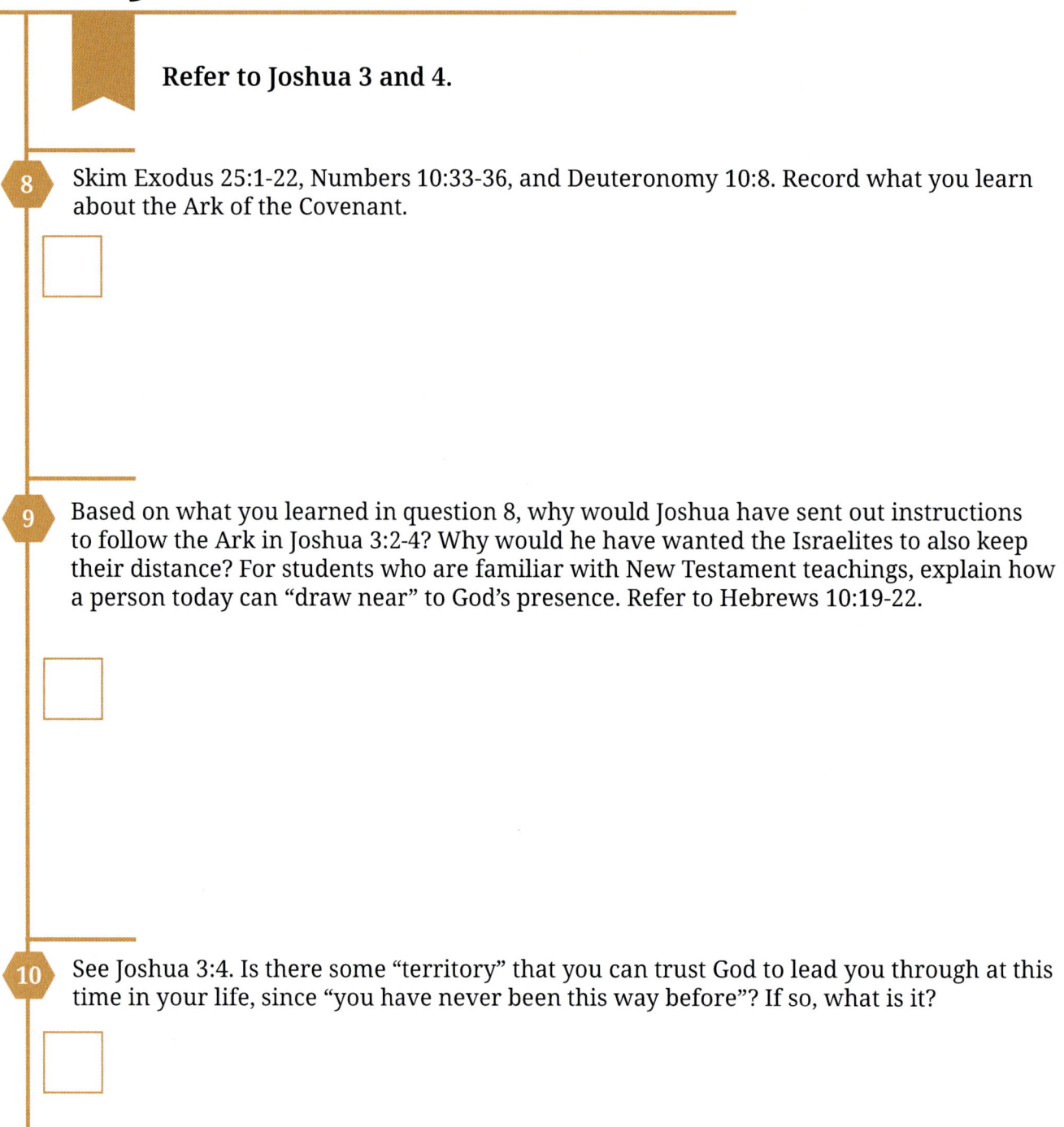

Refer to Joshua 3 and 4.

8. Skim Exodus 25:1-22, Numbers 10:33-36, and Deuteronomy 10:8. Record what you learn about the Ark of the Covenant.

9. Based on what you learned in question 8, why would Joshua have sent out instructions to follow the Ark in Joshua 3:2-4? Why would he have wanted the Israelites to also keep their distance? For students who are familiar with New Testament teachings, explain how a person today can "draw near" to God's presence. Refer to Hebrews 10:19-22.

10. See Joshua 3:4. Is there some "territory" that you can trust God to lead you through at this time in your life, since "you have never been this way before"? If so, what is it?

Day 4

Refer to Joshua 3 and 4.

11 List all the reasons why God miraculously stopped the flow of the Jordan River during its flood stage to allow the Israelites to cross on dry land.

12 Refer to Joshua 4:6 and 21. What has God done in your life recently that you ought to share with someone, so that they might delight in His awesome deeds? It does not need to be as dramatic as the crossing of the Jordan on dry ground!

Day 5

Refer to Joshua 5:1-12.

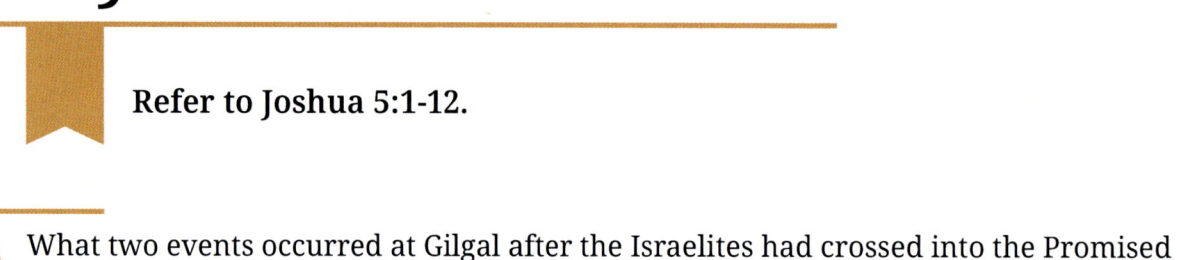

13 What two events occurred at Gilgal after the Israelites had crossed into the Promised Land but before they began to conquer it?

14 From Joshua 1:1-5:12, list all the events that should have prepared the Israelites for the conquest of the Promised Land. Explain your reasoning.

15 Reread Joshua 1:8. How does reading, meditating on, and obeying God's word prepare you for spiritual victory? Can you think of a way that it can help you gain victory this week?

Prayer Requests / Additional Notes

> **Spiritual victories are preceded by preparation.**

Point your phone camera here to view the Lesson 1 Video.

Preparation for Conquest
Closing Summary of Joshua 1:1-5:12

I. Introduction to the Book of Joshua

Principle: _____ ____ _____ _____ God's word are foundational to spiritual victory.

II. Reconnaissance and River Crossing - Joshua 2:1-5:1

Principle: Victorious Christian living requires _____.

III. Final Preparations - Joshua 5:2-12

Principle: A victorious life is the result of daily living out _____ _____.

31

Lesson Two

The Campaigns

Joshua 5:13-12:24

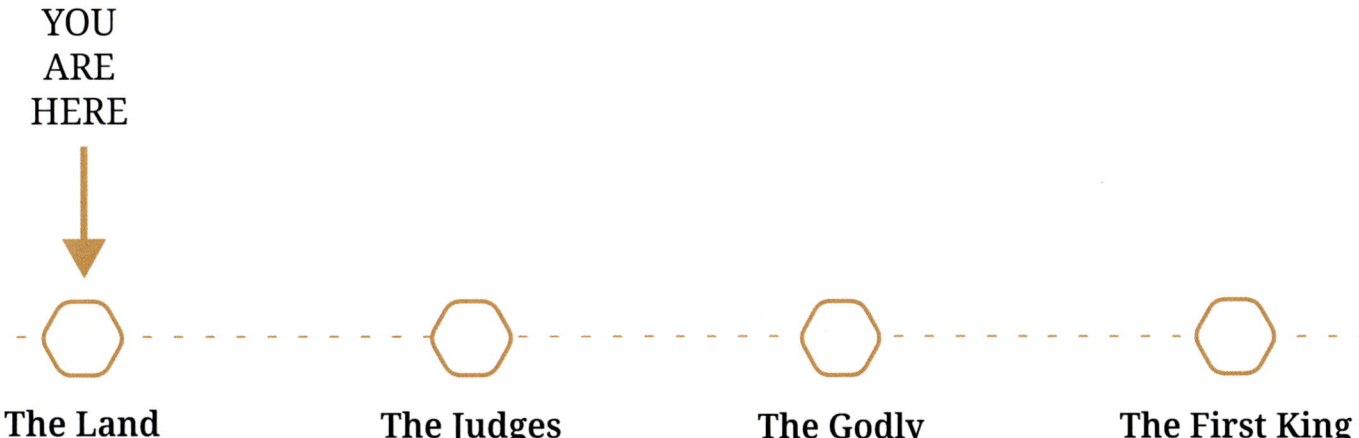

YOU ARE HERE ↓

○ The Land   ○ The Judges   ○ The Godly Remnant   ○ The First King

Day 1

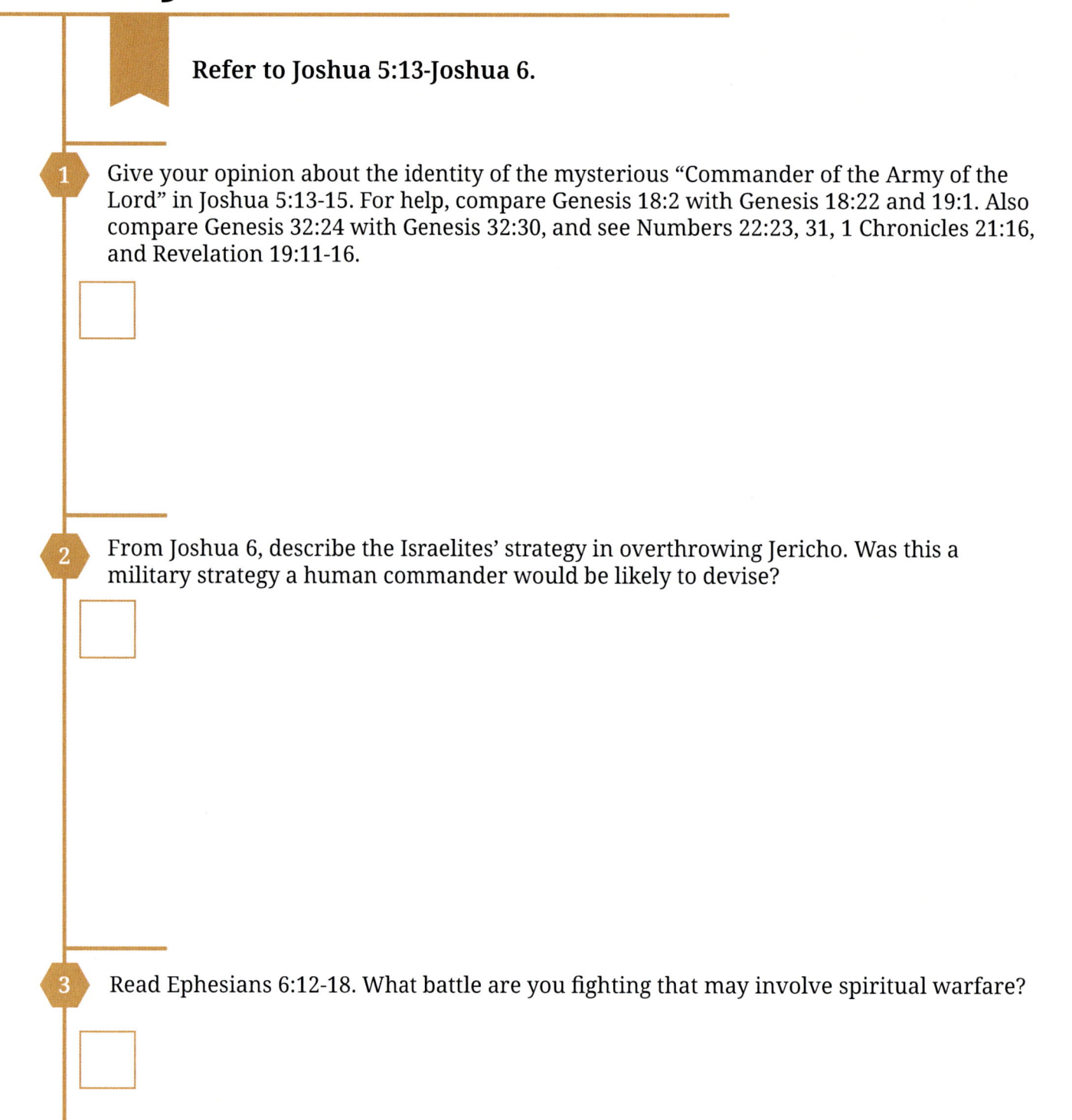

Refer to Joshua 5:13-Joshua 6.

1. Give your opinion about the identity of the mysterious "Commander of the Army of the Lord" in Joshua 5:13-15. For help, compare Genesis 18:2 with Genesis 18:22 and 19:1. Also compare Genesis 32:24 with Genesis 32:30, and see Numbers 22:23, 31, 1 Chronicles 21:16, and Revelation 19:11-16.

2. From Joshua 6, describe the Israelites' strategy in overthrowing Jericho. Was this a military strategy a human commander would be likely to devise?

3. Read Ephesians 6:12-18. What battle are you fighting that may involve spiritual warfare?

Day 2

Refer to Joshua 6.
The Beginning of Israel's Military Campaign in Central Canaan

4 Imagine being a resident of Jericho and observing the processional around the city day after day for seven days! What would have gone through your mind? See Joshua 2:8-13, 5:1.

5 According to Romans 1:18-20 and 2:14-16, by what means do all people possess certain knowledge about God? What further knowledge about God did the Canaanite/Amorite peoples possess? See Joshua 2:10 and 5:1.

6 From Leviticus 11:44-45, what is God's righteous standard? What is the deserved consequence of our sin according to Genesis 2:17-19, Romans 1:32, 5:12, 6:23, 8:13, Galatians 6:7-8, and James 1:15?

7 Revisit the following references from Lesson One and estimate the minimum number of years God patiently endured the Amorites' extreme depravity (sin): Genesis 15:13-16, Exodus 12:40-41, and Numbers 32:13.

8 It is difficult for us to think about the destruction of an entire city.

a Can you think of a reason why it was necessary, and perhaps even merciful, for God to order the deaths of the young along with the old? See Romans 2:6, Hebrews 4:13, 9:27, and Revelation 20:13.

b According to Romans 3:10-11, 23 and 1 Peter 3:18, who has ever deserved God's mercy and what provision has God made for our salvation?

c Read Titus 3:5. If you have experienced God's mercy and salvation through personal faith in Jesus Christ, how will you express your thanks to Him today? If you have not, what exactly is holding you back from receiving Jesus as your Savior and Lord this very moment? What assurance do you have that your life will not end and you will stand before God this very day?

Day 3

Refer to Joshua 6-8.
The Continuation of Israel's Military Campaign in Central Canaan

9 Skim Joshua 7 and 8. See especially 7:1-12, 20-21, 24-26 and 8:1-2, 20-22.

   a Explain the events that resulted in Israel's humiliating defeat at Ai.

   b Revisit Joshua 7:12. In what way does this verse explain the problem? What specifically did God say He required of Israel in order that He would be with them and grant them victory against Ai?

10 Read Joshua 8:30-35 with Deuteronomy 27:1-13 and 28:1-2, 15. After Israel occupied key cities in central Canaan, they renewed their covenant with the Lord as Moses had instructed. According to the verses in Deuteronomy 28, why was it important for Joshua to recite the book of the Law in the presence of all Israel?

11 Read 1 John 1:8-2:6. In light of the passage, what attitudes toward sin and obedience should characterize believers? Do you currently need to adjust any of your attitudes?

Day 4

Refer to Joshua 9.

12. Read Joshua 9:1-6, 14-27. What does verse 24 reveal about the degree to which the Gibeonites understood who ordered their destruction?

13. What explanation for Israel's failure with regard to the Gibeonites is given in Joshua 9:14? Is there a matter you have recently considered too unimportant or unnecessary to pray about and assumed your own good judgment would suffice?

Day 5

Refer to Joshua 10-12.
Israel's Southern and Northern Military Campaigns in Canaan

14 Read Joshua 10:1-15, 42 and 11:1-8, 15. Using these verses, summarize Joshua's campaigns in southern and northern Canaan.

15 Reread Joshua 10:9-14.

a. How do these verses illustrate the interplay between human effort and divine involvement?

b. What effort is currently being demanded of you that you will trust God to divinely oversee?

Prayer Requests / Additional Notes

Joshua's Campaigns

- ▲ Philistine Cities
- ✹ Cities of Refuge
- • Other Cities
- — 1st Campaign
- — 2nd Campaign
- — 3rd Campaign

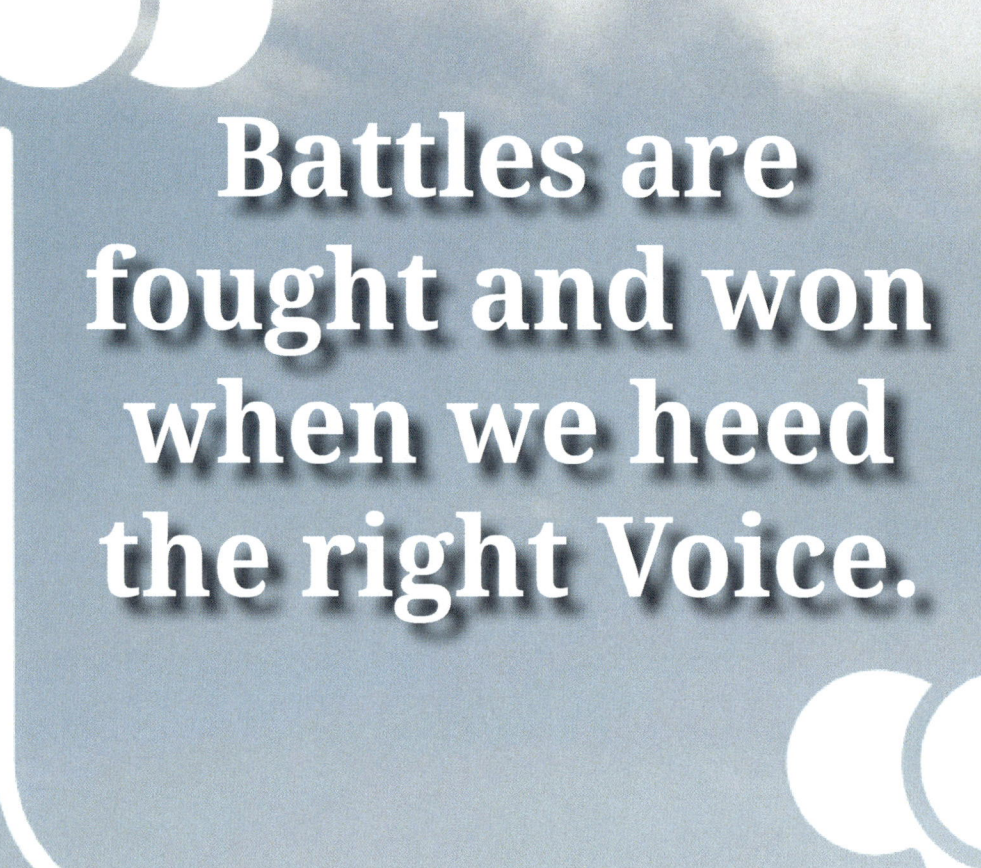

"Battles are fought and won when we heed the right Voice."

Point your phone camera here to view the Lesson 2 Video.

The Campaigns
Closing Summary of Joshua 5:13-12:24

I. Central Campaign Launched - Joshua 5:13-Joshua 6

Principle: God's instructions _____ _____ human logic.

II. Central Campaign Completed - Joshua 7-9

Principle: Constant alertness to dangers prevents us from being lulled into a _____ _____ ____ _____ and a resulting attitude of self-reliance.

III. Southern and Northern Campaigns - Joshua 10-12

Principle: "The Lord has not given us a _____ ____ _____" (2 Timothy 1:7).

Lesson Three

Division of the Land

Joshua 13-24

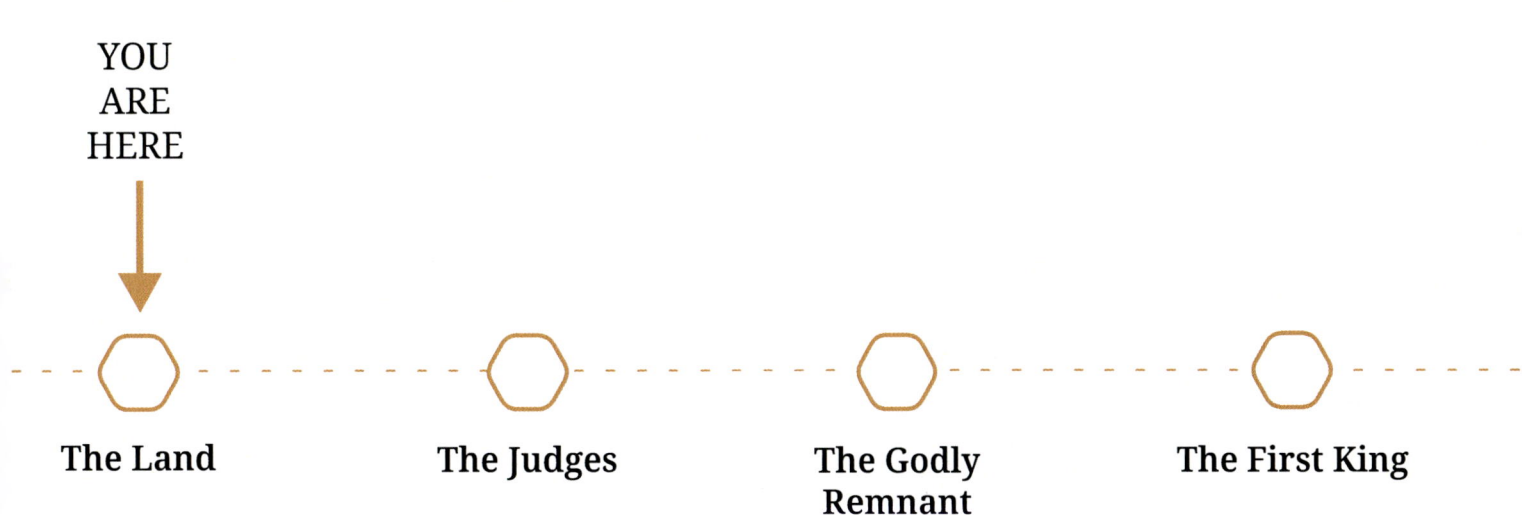

YOU
ARE
HERE

○   ○   ○   ○

The Land   The Judges   The Godly Remnant   The First King

Day 1

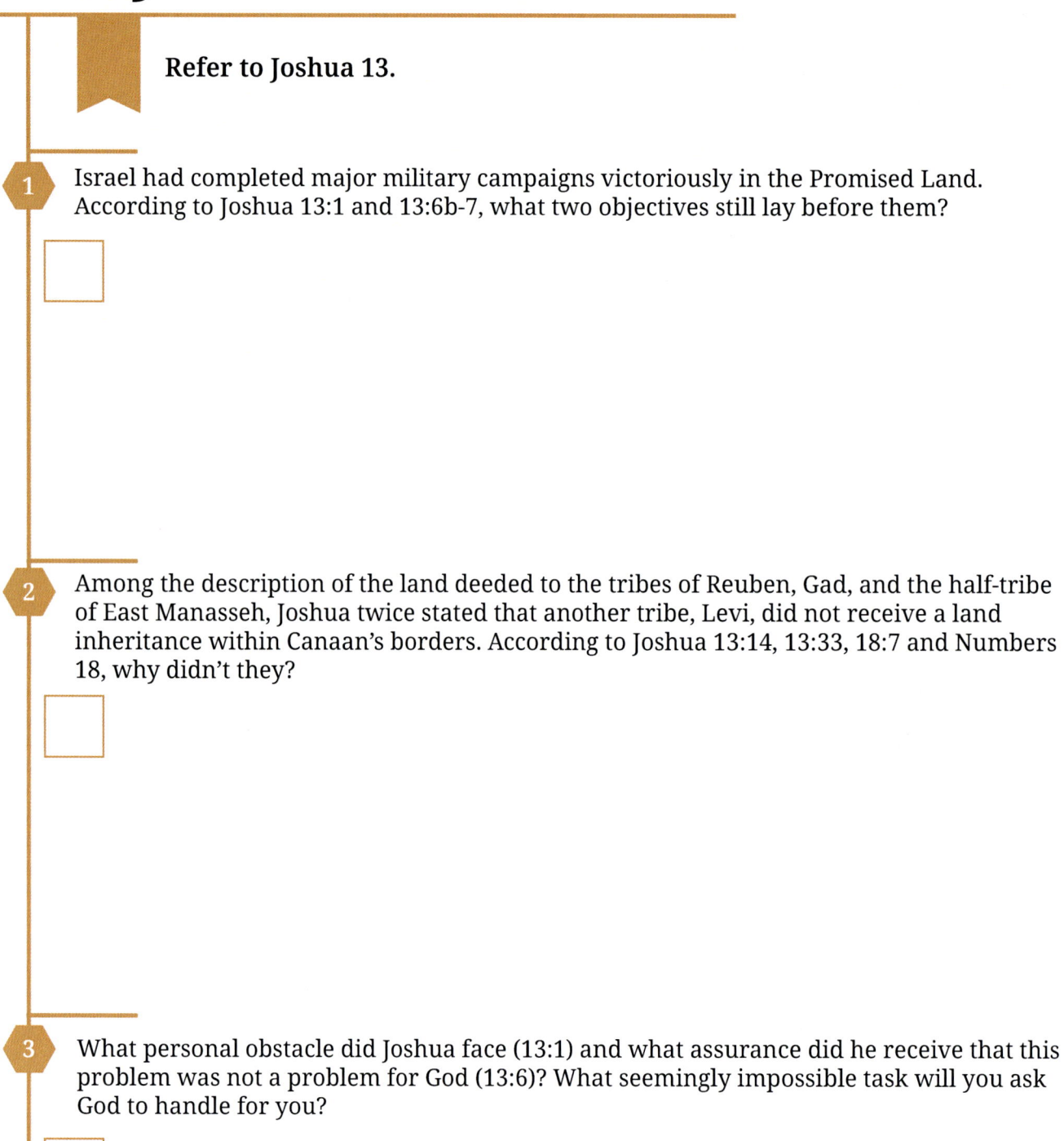

Refer to Joshua 13.

1. Israel had completed major military campaigns victoriously in the Promised Land. According to Joshua 13:1 and 13:6b-7, what two objectives still lay before them?

2. Among the description of the land deeded to the tribes of Reuben, Gad, and the half-tribe of East Manasseh, Joshua twice stated that another tribe, Levi, did not receive a land inheritance within Canaan's borders. According to Joshua 13:14, 13:33, 18:7 and Numbers 18, why didn't they?

3. What personal obstacle did Joshua face (13:1) and what assurance did he receive that this problem was not a problem for God (13:6)? What seemingly impossible task will you ask God to handle for you?

Day 2

Refer to Joshua 14-19.

4 Joshua 14-19 records the tracts of land deeded to the remaining nine-and-a-half tribes west of the Jordan in Canaan. Based on any knowledge you have about the first five books of the Bible, why were the recording of these deeds and the receiving of the land causes for great rejoicing in Israel?

5 Read Numbers 14:6-25, and then skim Numbers 13 and 14:26-38 for information about Caleb. According to Numbers 14:30 and Joshua 14:10-11, what promise did God make and fulfill, and how did He bless Caleb even beyond what He had promised?

6 Compare Caleb's courageous expansion of his territory (Joshua 15:13-19) to Ephraim and Manasseh's complaint that they were unable to take all their land (Joshua 17:14-18). Then, summarize Joshua's advice in Joshua 17:18b. Which person who depends on you for advice, guidance, or leadership could you similarly encourage?

7 Keeping in mind what you learned about the attitude of the tribes of Joseph (Ephraim and Manasseh) in question 6, read Joshua 15:63, 16:10, and 17:12-13.

   a What danger was war-weary Israel succumbing to and with what likely result? See Joshua 23:12-13.

   b Is there a stronghold of sin that you have dismissed as too difficult to dislodge from your life or not worth the effort? What does Philippians 1:6 say to encourage you?

47

Day 3

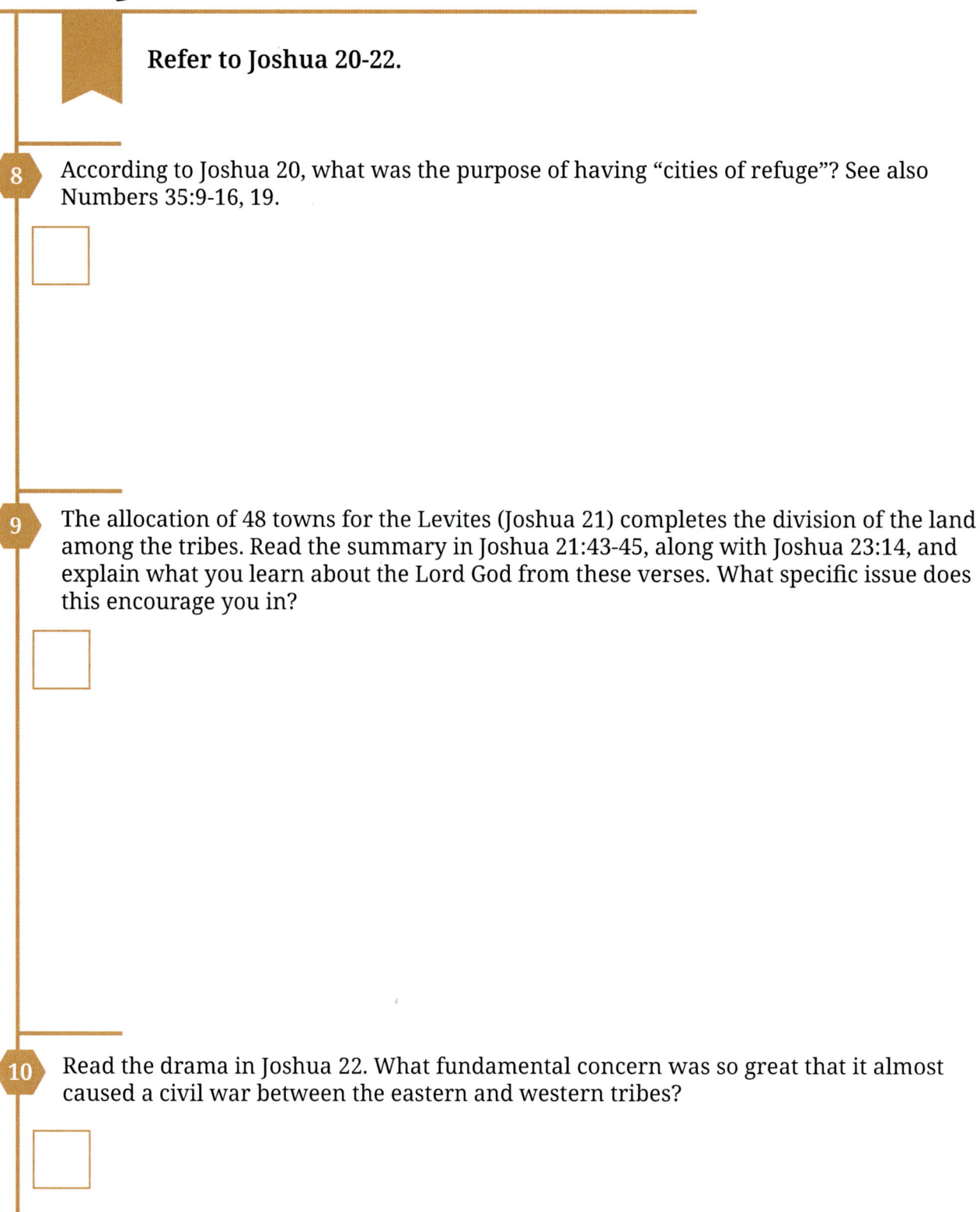

Refer to Joshua 20-22.

8 According to Joshua 20, what was the purpose of having "cities of refuge"? See also Numbers 35:9-16, 19.

9 The allocation of 48 towns for the Levites (Joshua 21) completes the division of the land among the tribes. Read the summary in Joshua 21:43-45, along with Joshua 23:14, and explain what you learn about the Lord God from these verses. What specific issue does this encourage you in?

10 Read the drama in Joshua 22. What fundamental concern was so great that it almost caused a civil war between the eastern and western tribes?

Day 4

Refer to Joshua 23-24.

11 List the instructions and warnings Joshua gave Israel at the end of his life (chapter 23).

12 According to Joshua 24, Joshua summoned the Israelites to renew their covenant agreement with God. What was the significance of choosing Shechem as the site for the ceremony? See Genesis 12:6-7. According to Joshua 24:32, what other significant event took place at Shechem, presumably during Joshua's lifetime?

13 According to Joshua 24, what choice did Israel face? Include verse numbers. Specifically, how does this same choice challenge your life today?

Day 5

Refer to Joshua 24.

14 Which phrase in Joshua 24:31 explains Israel's faithfulness during the years Joshua's contemporaries remained alive?

15 What have you personally witnessed the Lord do for you that you need to share with your spiritual and physical descendants?

Prayer Requests / Additional Notes

TRIBAL DIVISION OF CANAAN
ARAM
Damascus
Litani River
SYRIA
Tyre
KADESH
DAN
ASHER
NAPHTALI
EAST MANASSEH
SEA OF GALILEE
Rimmon
ZEBULUN
Golan
MEDITERRANEAN SEA
Yarmuk River
ISSACHAR
Megiddo
Jezreel
Remoth Gilead
Jabesh (Gilead)
WEST MANASSEH
Samaria
Tirzah
Shecem
Mahanaim
Jordan River
Jabbok River
AMMON
GAD
Joppa
EPHRAIM
Shiloh
Ramoth
Bethel
Mizpah
Gilgal
DAN
Gibeon
Jericho
Bezer
Ekron
Ashdod
Kiriath Jearim
Jerusalem
BENJAMIN
Gath
Bethlehem
Ashkelon
JUDAH
REUBEN
Hebron
Gaza
DEAD SEA
Arnon River
Beersheba
MOAB
SIMEON
Philistine Cities
Cities of Refuge
Other Cities
Zerod River
EDOM

> The "Promised Land" is the place of greatest spiritual blessing this side of Heaven.

Point your phone camera here to view the Lesson 3 Video.

Division of the Land
Closing Summary of Joshua 13-24

I. Allotment of the Land - Joshua 13-19

Principle: Promised Land dwellers experience the thrill of discovering that the indwelling Holy Spirit is the _____ _____ _____.

II. Designation of Special Cities - Joshua 20-21

Principle: Promised Land dwellers experience the joy of discovering that _____ _____ is their inheritance.

III. Conflict and Commitment - Joshua 22-24

Principle: Promised Land dwellers experience the blessing of discovering they have a _____ _____.

Lesson Four

Causes of Israel's Decline, Deborah, Gideon

Judges 1-9

YOU ARE HERE

The Land — The Judges — The Godly Remnant — The First King

Day 1

Refer to Judges 1-2.
Causes of Israel's Decline

1. Read what Judges 1:1-3 and Joshua 19:1 say about the tribes of Judah and Simeon. Then, look back at Jacob's prophetic blessings over his twelve sons on his deathbed (Genesis 49). Explain how Judges 1:2-3 reveals a partial fulfillment of the prophecies about Judah and Simeon (Genesis 49:5-12).

2. Following the national campaigns that Joshua fought and won, Judges 1 reveals information about regional tribal battles that were fought to drive remaining inhabitants out of the Promised Land. How thoroughly did Israel cleanse the land of these people groups? See Judges 1:19, 21, 27-36 and 2:2-5.

3. Judges 2:10-19 describes a cycle of apostasy (abandoning faith in God) that characterized Israel during the period of the Judges.

    a) Use the verses listed to fill in the missing words:

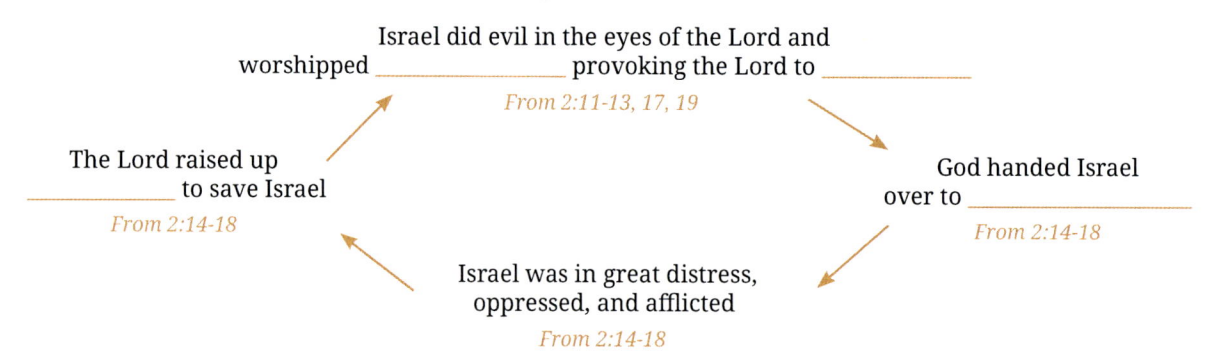

    Israel did evil in the eyes of the Lord and worshipped _____ provoking the Lord to _____
    From 2:11-13, 17, 19

    God handed Israel over to _____
    From 2:14-18

    Israel was in great distress, oppressed, and afflicted
    From 2:14-18

    The Lord raised up _____ to save Israel
    From 2:14-18

    b) What does 2:10-19 reveal about God's anger toward the Israelites?

    c) What does 2:10-19 reveal about God's mercy toward the Israelites?

    d) Which behaviors of the Israelites, as described in 2:10-19, are typical of people in every era who neither "know the Lord nor what He has done" (2:10)?

    e) How will you use what you learn from this cycle to intercede in prayer for yourself or others?

Day 2

Refer to Judges 2-3.
Causes of Israel's Decline

4 What reasons did God give for allowing the other nations to be left in the land after Joshua's death? See Judges 2:20-3:6.

5 See any text note in your Bible that clarifies the word translated "judge," for example, in Judges 2:16. What insight about the nature of this office is given in Judges 2:16, 18 and 3:9-10, 15-16, 31?

6 Israel had many enemies.

  a Which three enemies of the Israelites are named in Judges 3:7-31 and who were the first three judges the Lord raised up to deliver Israel from them? Include verse numbers.

  b From Judges 4:2, 6:1-3, and 10:7, list the names of Israel's other enemies in this period.

  c What kind of personal, social, or spiritual enemies do you need to ask the Lord to deliver you from today? See John 15:18, Romans 8:8, and 1 Peter 5:8.

Day 3

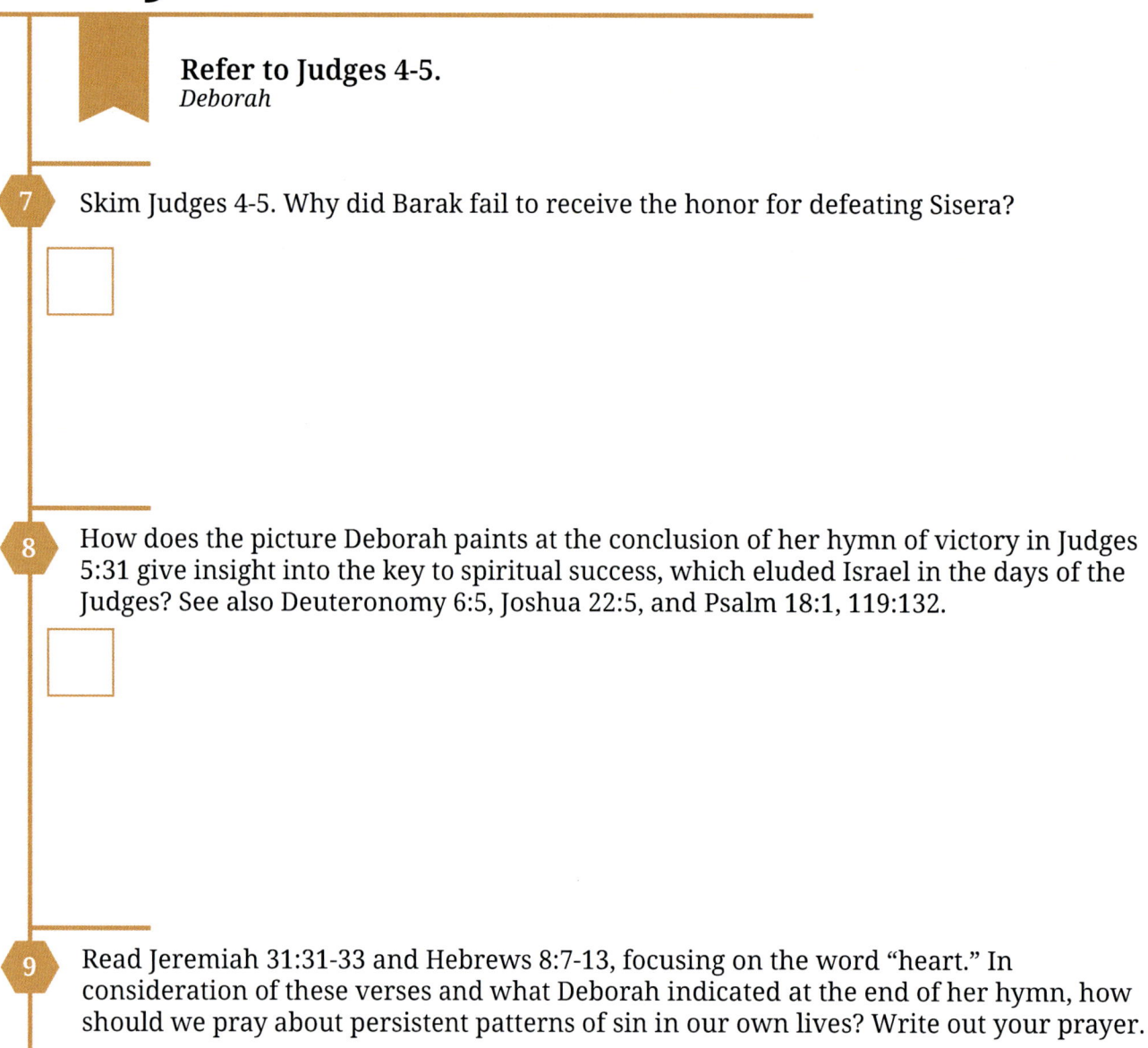

Refer to Judges 4-5.
Deborah

7 Skim Judges 4-5. Why did Barak fail to receive the honor for defeating Sisera?

8 How does the picture Deborah paints at the conclusion of her hymn of victory in Judges 5:31 give insight into the key to spiritual success, which eluded Israel in the days of the Judges? See also Deuteronomy 6:5, Joshua 22:5, and Psalm 18:1, 119:132.

9 Read Jeremiah 31:31-33 and Hebrews 8:7-13, focusing on the word "heart." In consideration of these verses and what Deborah indicated at the end of her hymn, how should we pray about persistent patterns of sin in our own lives? Write out your prayer.

Day 4

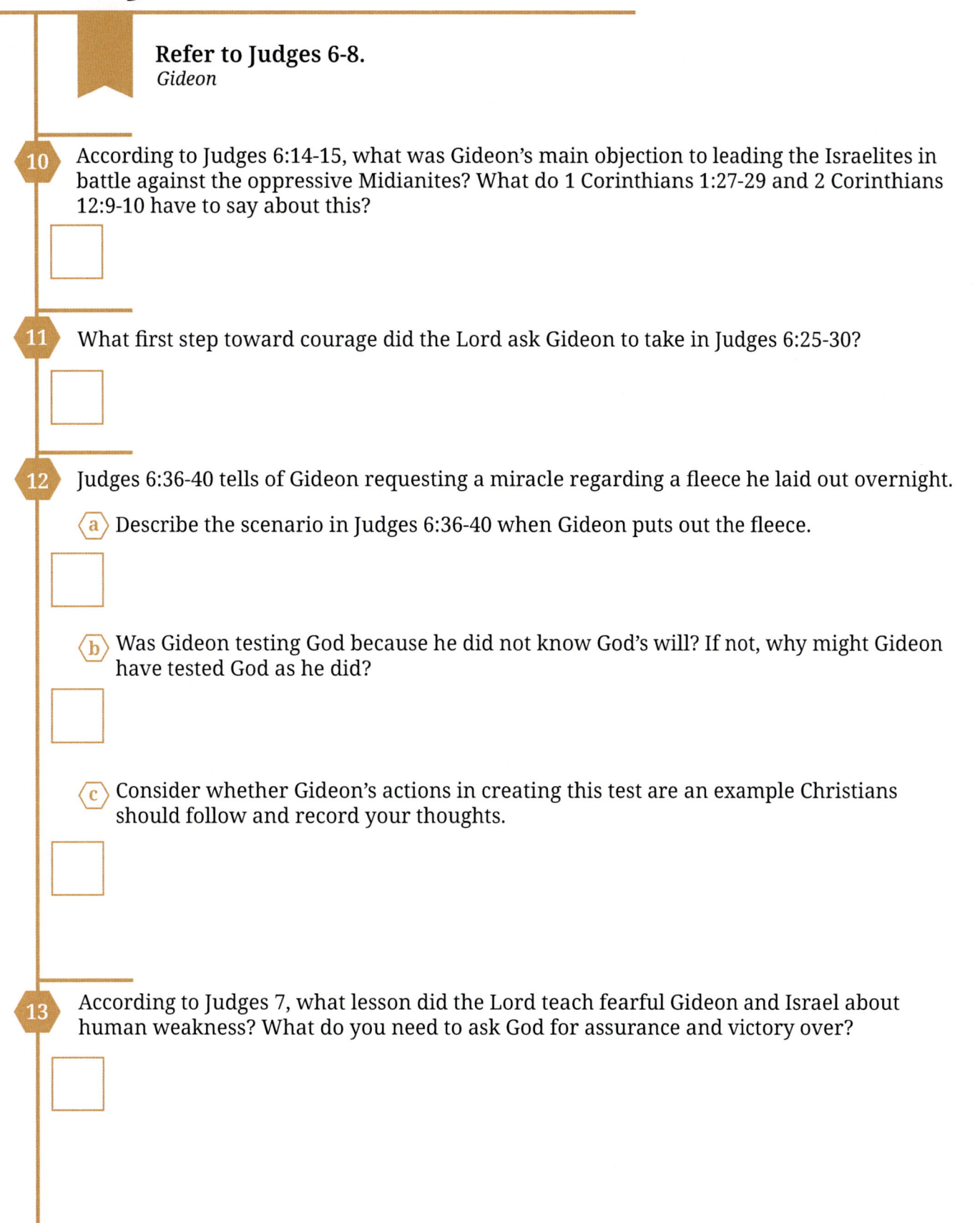

Refer to Judges 6-8.
Gideon

10 According to Judges 6:14-15, what was Gideon's main objection to leading the Israelites in battle against the oppressive Midianites? What do 1 Corinthians 1:27-29 and 2 Corinthians 12:9-10 have to say about this?

11 What first step toward courage did the Lord ask Gideon to take in Judges 6:25-30?

12 Judges 6:36-40 tells of Gideon requesting a miracle regarding a fleece he laid out overnight.

a Describe the scenario in Judges 6:36-40 when Gideon puts out the fleece.

b Was Gideon testing God because he did not know God's will? If not, why might Gideon have tested God as he did?

c Consider whether Gideon's actions in creating this test are an example Christians should follow and record your thoughts.

13 According to Judges 7, what lesson did the Lord teach fearful Gideon and Israel about human weakness? What do you need to ask God for assurance and victory over?

61

Day 5

Refer to Judges 8-9.
Gideon's Son Abimelech

14 Read Judges 8:22-23, 29-31 with 9:1-6, 22-24, 42-57. What did Gideon's son Abimelech desire for himself?

15 Compare Gideon's declaration about the Lord in Judges 8:23 with the Israelites' attitude toward the Lord in the period of the Judges. See Judges 1-2 and review your answers to questions 2-3 if necessary. Read Revelation 19:16. Specifically, what will you change or do differently today in acknowledgment of Jesus' rightful lordship?

Prayer Requests / Additional Notes

> We are in trouble when we become comfortable with the progress we have made and gradually stop doing all that we should.

Point your phone camera here to view the Lesson 4 Video.

Causes of Israel's Decline, Deborah, Gideon

Closing Summary of Judges 1-9

I. Introduction to Judges and the Cycle of Apostasy - Judges 1:1-6:6

Principle: We _____ what we value the most.

II. Illustrations of the Cycle of Apostasy - Judges 3:7-9:57

Principle: Small sins lead to _____ _____.

65

Lesson Five

Jephthah, Samson, Consequences of Decline

Judges 10-21

YOU
ARE
HERE

The Land — The Judges — The Godly Remnant — The First King

Day 1

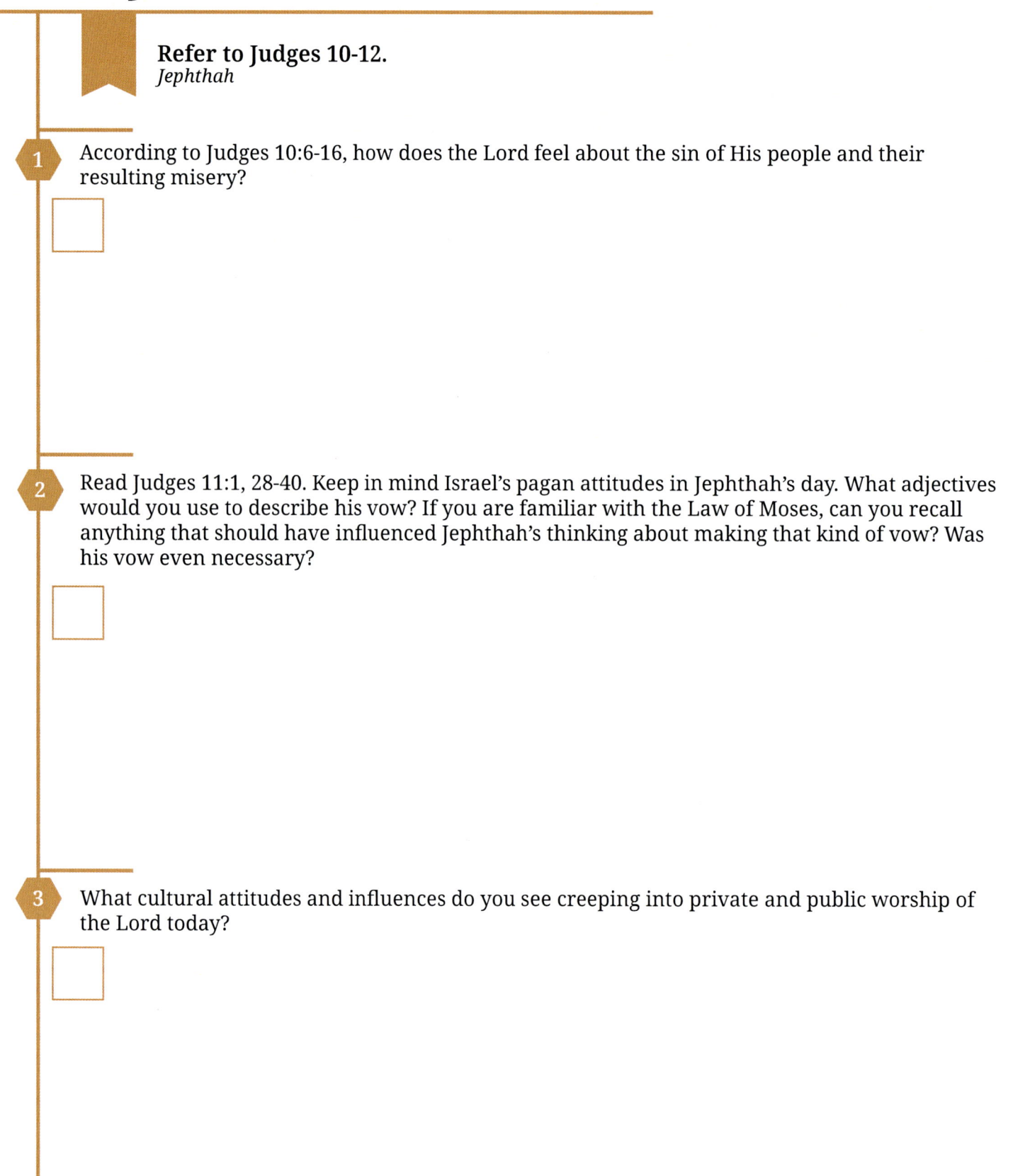

Refer to Judges 10-12.
Jephthah

1 According to Judges 10:6-16, how does the Lord feel about the sin of His people and their resulting misery?

2 Read Judges 11:1, 28-40. Keep in mind Israel's pagan attitudes in Jephthah's day. What adjectives would you use to describe his vow? If you are familiar with the Law of Moses, can you recall anything that should have influenced Jephthah's thinking about making that kind of vow? Was his vow even necessary?

3 What cultural attitudes and influences do you see creeping into private and public worship of the Lord today?

Day 2

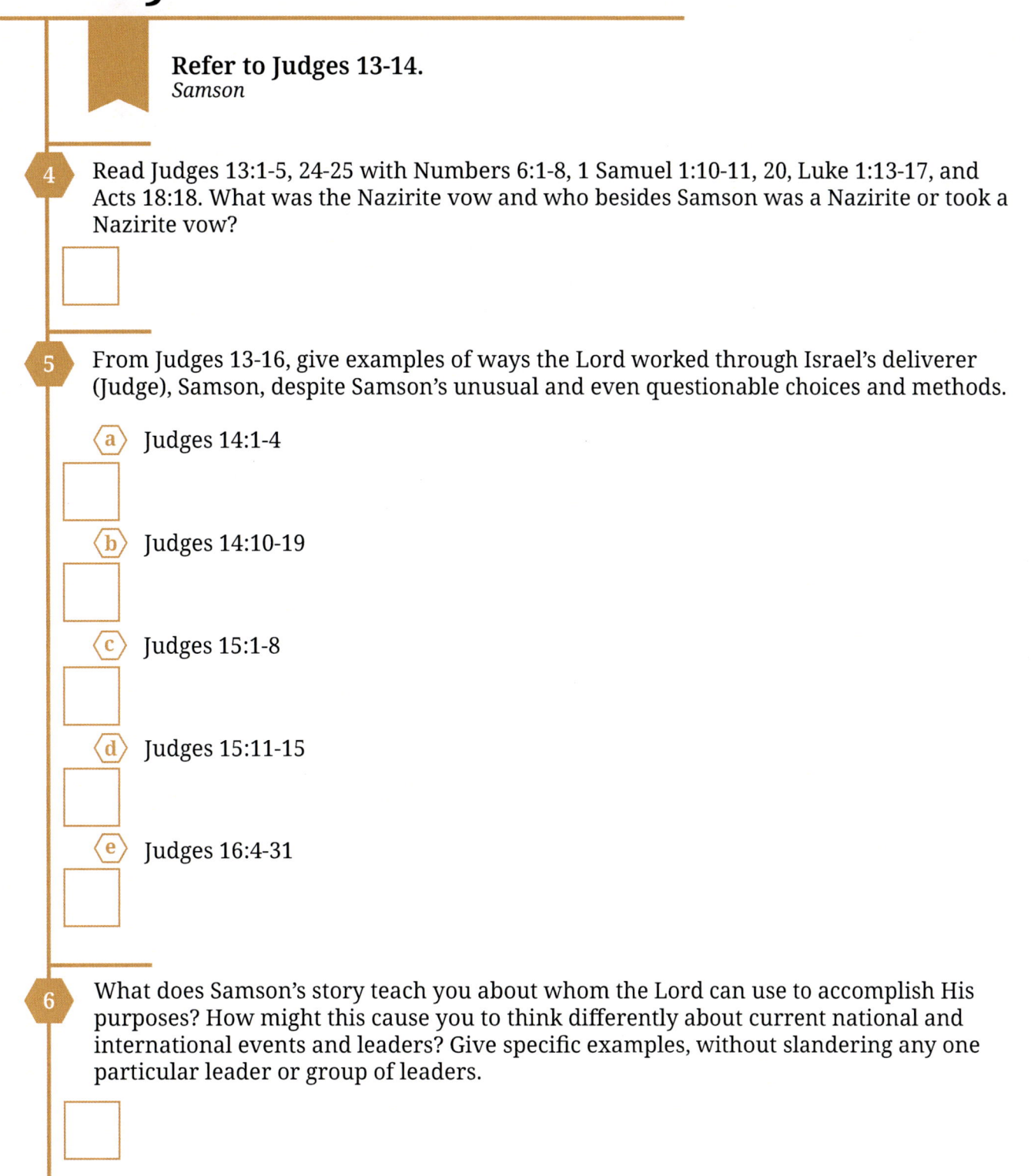

Refer to Judges 13-14.
Samson

4 Read Judges 13:1-5, 24-25 with Numbers 6:1-8, 1 Samuel 1:10-11, 20, Luke 1:13-17, and Acts 18:18. What was the Nazirite vow and who besides Samson was a Nazirite or took a Nazirite vow?

5 From Judges 13-16, give examples of ways the Lord worked through Israel's deliverer (Judge), Samson, despite Samson's unusual and even questionable choices and methods.

  a Judges 14:1-4

  b Judges 14:10-19

  c Judges 15:1-8

  d Judges 15:11-15

  e Judges 16:4-31

6 What does Samson's story teach you about whom the Lord can use to accomplish His purposes? How might this cause you to think differently about current national and international events and leaders? Give specific examples, without slandering any one particular leader or group of leaders.

Day 3

Refer to Judges 17-18.
Micah's Priest and the Danites

7 What signs of spiritual chaos can you find in the following verses?

a Judges 17:3-4 (See Exodus 20:4.)

b Judges 17:1, 5 and 10-12 (See Exodus 40:12-15 and Numbers 18:1, 7.)
Note: Although Aaron and his sons descended from the line of Levi, under the Mosaic law, only Aaron's descendants had the right to be priests, not the Levites in general.

c Judges 17:13

d Judges 18:1-6, 27, 30-31

8 At first, we may find Israel's sins incomprehensible. They were God's own people! What does 1 Corinthians 10:1-13 say about this? What specific warning do you need to take from this period in Israel's history?

Day 4

Refer to Judges 19-21.
Civil War in Israel

9. Read Judges 19. Which verses bear a striking resemblance to Genesis 19:4-8? Since the writer of Judges almost certainly assumed his readers would be familiar with Genesis, what point about Israel's moral condition was he making?

10. Why did the Levite gruesomely cut his dead concubine's body into twelve pieces?

11. Judges 20 describes a very dark hour in Israel's history that resulted from the murder of the Levite's concubine (chapter 19).

    a) According to Judges 20:8-11, what verdict did Israel render upon the tribe of Benjamin?

    b) Summarize the events that followed in verses 20-21, 24-29, 35-36, and 48.

12. According to Judges 21, how did Israel ensure the tribe of Benjamin was not altogether erased?

13. Read Judges 17:6 and 21:25. How does this summary of Israel's condition compare to the moral climate in your own culture? What can you personally do to keep such thinking from prevailing among believers in your area?

Day 5

Refer to the book of Judges.

14 According to Judges 8:1, 12:1-4, and 20:18-48, what politically significant consequence resulted from Israel's spiritual decline?

☐

15 Read Romans 15:5-6. Are you in a relationship or group in which an absence of true spirituality is fostering disunity? If so, what can you do about it?

☐

Prayer Requests / Additional Notes

> Living by our own foolish "wisdom" results in personal and social disaster.

Point your phone camera here to view the Lesson 5 Video.

Jephthah, Samson, Consequences of Decline
Closing Summary of Judges 10-21

I. Jephthah and Five "Minor" Judges - Judges 10-12

Principle: _____ _____ _____ is unnecessary and can end in disappointment.

II. Samson - Judges 13-16

Principle: Living according to our _____ is perilous.

III. Internal Threats Illustrated - Judges 17-21

Principle: As goes the _____, so goes the _____.

Lesson Six

Naomi's Story

Ruth 1-4

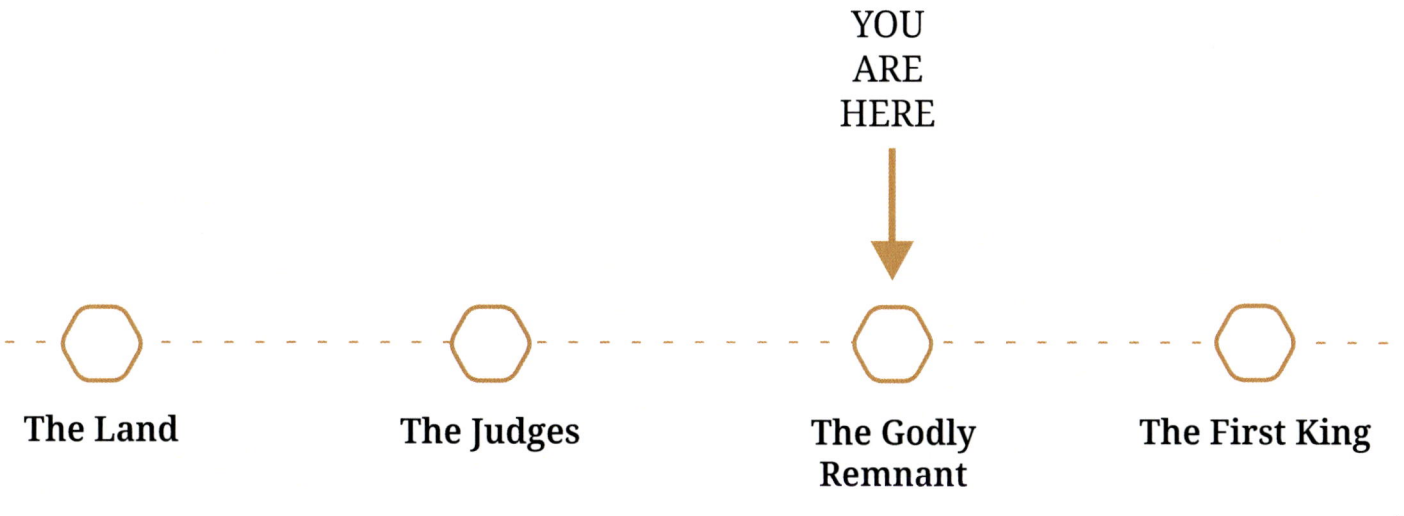

YOU ARE HERE ↓

The Land — The Judges — The Godly Remnant — The First King

Day 1

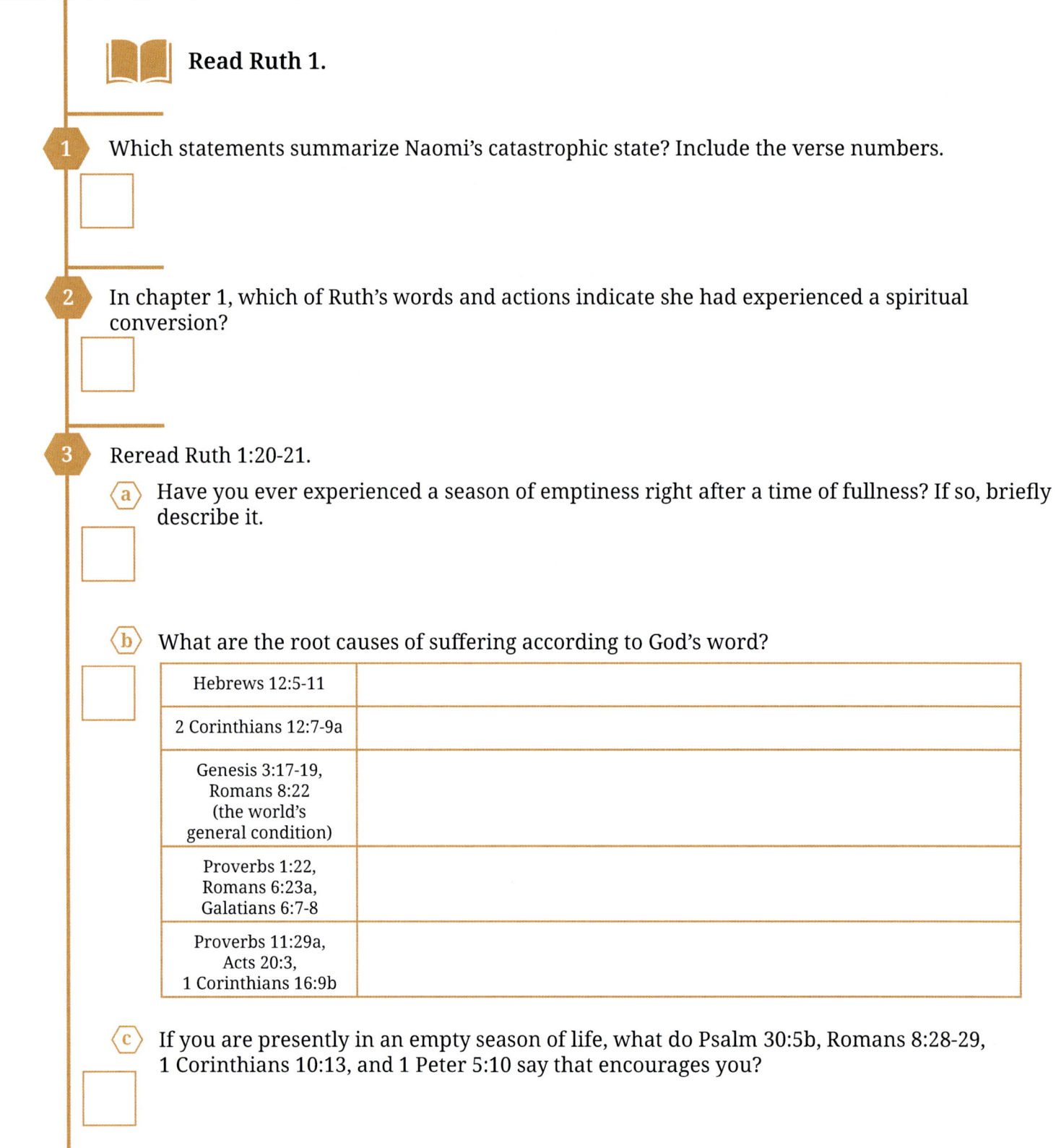

Read Ruth 1.

1 Which statements summarize Naomi's catastrophic state? Include the verse numbers.

2 In chapter 1, which of Ruth's words and actions indicate she had experienced a spiritual conversion?

3 Reread Ruth 1:20-21.

a Have you ever experienced a season of emptiness right after a time of fullness? If so, briefly describe it.

b What are the root causes of suffering according to God's word?

Hebrews 12:5-11	
2 Corinthians 12:7-9a	
Genesis 3:17-19, Romans 8:22 (the world's general condition)	
Proverbs 1:22, Romans 6:23a, Galatians 6:7-8	
Proverbs 11:29a, Acts 20:3, 1 Corinthians 16:9b	

c If you are presently in an empty season of life, what do Psalm 30:5b, Romans 8:28-29, 1 Corinthians 10:13, and 1 Peter 5:10 say that encourages you?

Day 2

📖 **Read Ruth 2.**

4 In what verses and phrases of Ruth 2 do you see God at work behind the scenes?

5 What character qualities of Ruth and Boaz does chapter 2 reveal?

6 Boaz was a blessing to Ruth and Ruth was a blessing to Naomi. Who has God placed in your life that you could seek to bless? What specific steps will you take this week?

Day 3

📖 **Read Ruth 3.**

7 Summarize Naomi's plan as described in Ruth 3. In what ways would this plan have been risky for Ruth?

8 What was Boaz's response to Ruth's initiative?

9 What "faith-risk" is God asking you to take right now?

Day 4

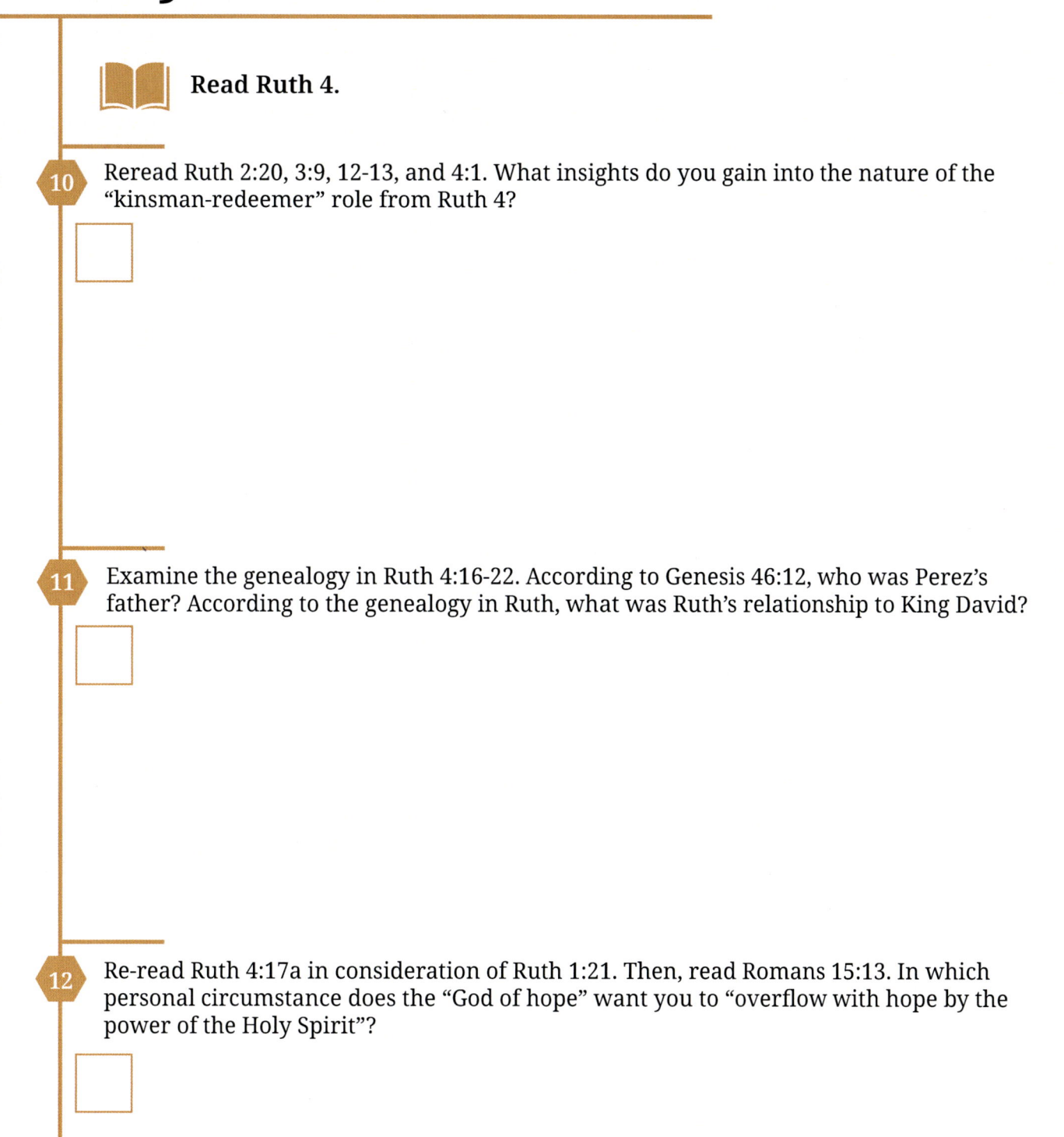

📖 **Read Ruth 4.**

10 Reread Ruth 2:20, 3:9, 12-13, and 4:1. What insights do you gain into the nature of the "kinsman-redeemer" role from Ruth 4?

11 Examine the genealogy in Ruth 4:16-22. According to Genesis 46:12, who was Perez's father? According to the genealogy in Ruth, what was Ruth's relationship to King David?

12 Re-read Ruth 4:17a in consideration of Ruth 1:21. Then, read Romans 15:13. In which personal circumstance does the "God of hope" want you to "overflow with hope by the power of the Holy Spirit"?

Day 5

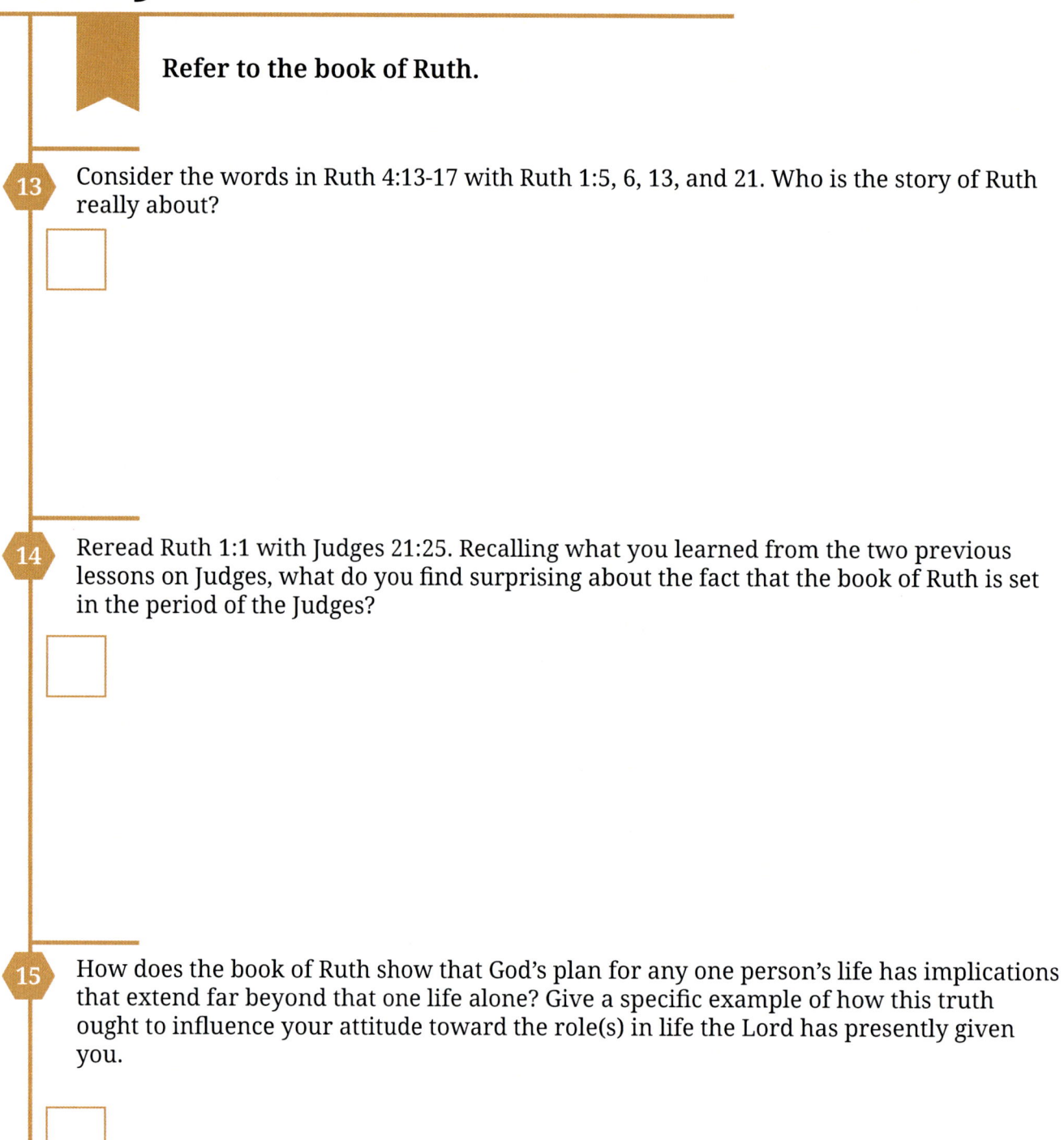

Refer to the book of Ruth.

13 Consider the words in Ruth 4:13-17 with Ruth 1:5, 6, 13, and 21. Who is the story of Ruth really about?

14 Reread Ruth 1:1 with Judges 21:25. Recalling what you learned from the two previous lessons on Judges, what do you find surprising about the fact that the book of Ruth is set in the period of the Judges?

15 How does the book of Ruth show that God's plan for any one person's life has implications that extend far beyond that one life alone? Give a specific example of how this truth ought to influence your attitude toward the role(s) in life the Lord has presently given you.

Prayer Requests / Additional Notes

"God is always at work behind the scenes."

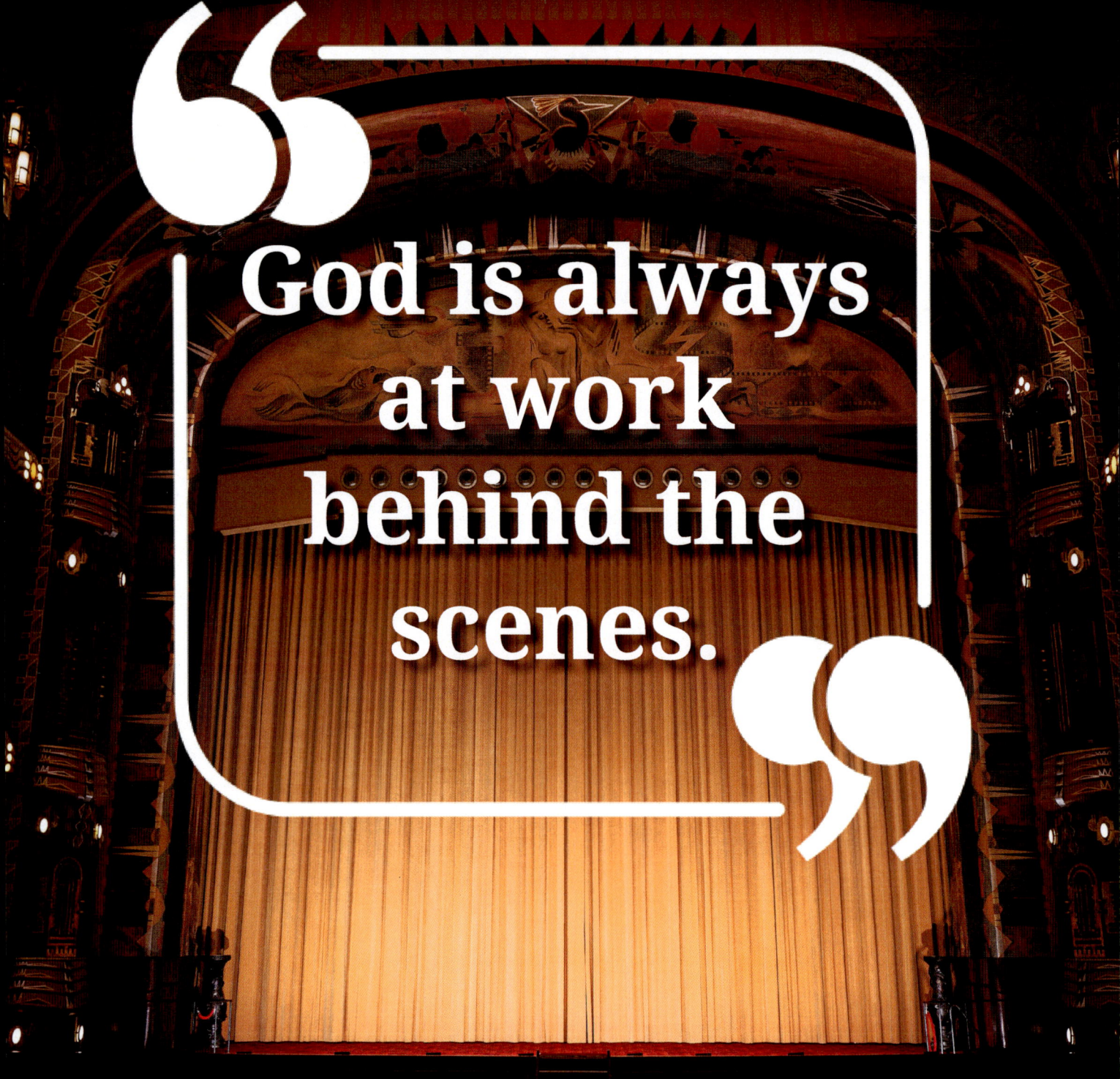

Point your phone camera here to view the Lesson 6 Video.

Naomi's Story
Closing Summary of Ruth 1-4

I. Naomi's Problems - Ruth 1

Principle: Viewing our circumstances with _____ _____ renews our perspective.

II. A Providential Encounter - Ruth 2

Principle: When we _____ "_____" to hurting people, they are sometimes awakened to God's providential involvement in their lives.

III. Several Bold Initiatives - Ruth 3-4

Principle: God's plan for each believer's life _____ _____ _____ the impact to him or her alone.

85

Lesson Seven

Samuel's Birth and Call

1 Samuel 1-3

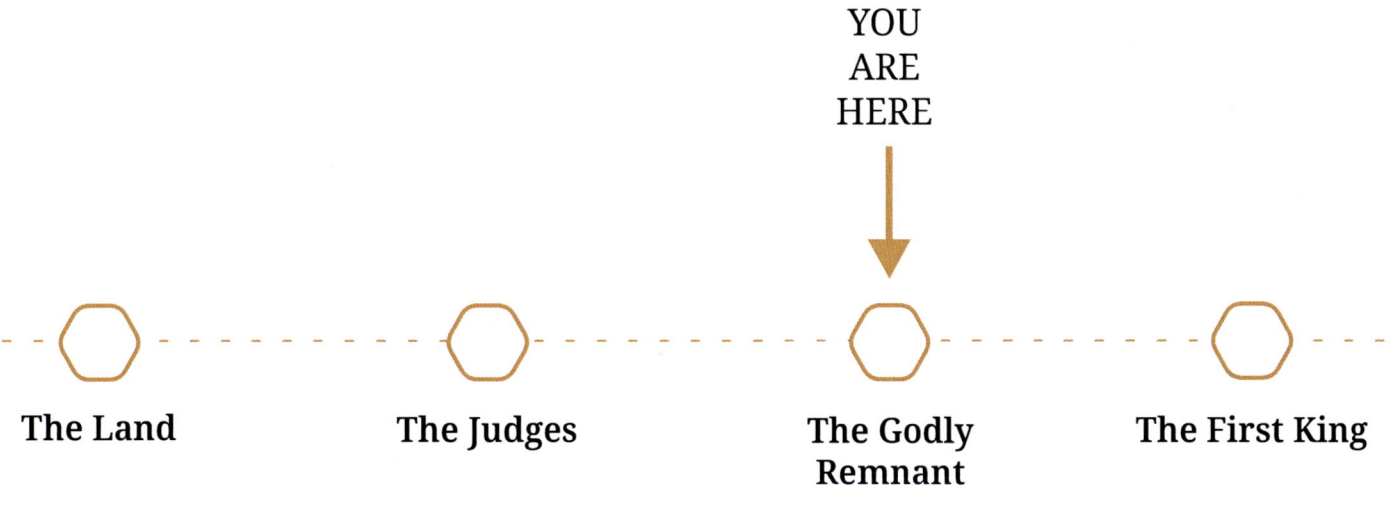

YOU ARE HERE
↓

The Land — The Judges — The Godly Remnant — The First King

Day 1

📖 **Read 1 Samuel 1.**

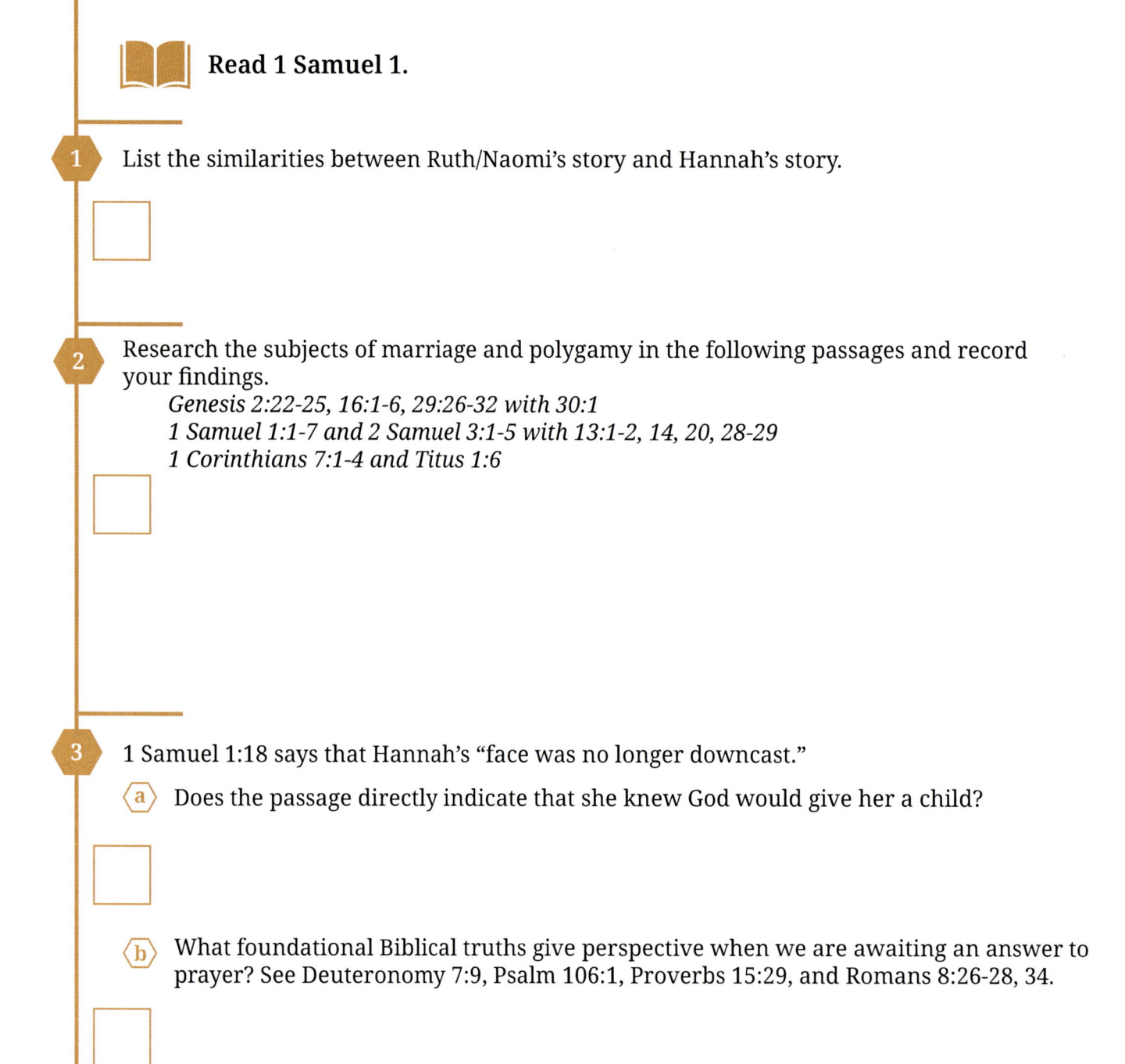

1 List the similarities between Ruth/Naomi's story and Hannah's story.

2 Research the subjects of marriage and polygamy in the following passages and record your findings.
   Genesis 2:22-25, 16:1-6, 29:26-32 with 30:1
   1 Samuel 1:1-7 and 2 Samuel 3:1-5 with 13:1-2, 14, 20, 28-29
   1 Corinthians 7:1-4 and Titus 1:6

3 1 Samuel 1:18 says that Hannah's "face was no longer downcast."

   a Does the passage directly indicate that she knew God would give her a child?

   b What foundational Biblical truths give perspective when we are awaiting an answer to prayer? See Deuteronomy 7:9, Psalm 106:1, Proverbs 15:29, and Romans 8:26-28, 34.

   c With regard to which yet unanswered prayer do you need this Biblical perspective?

Day 2

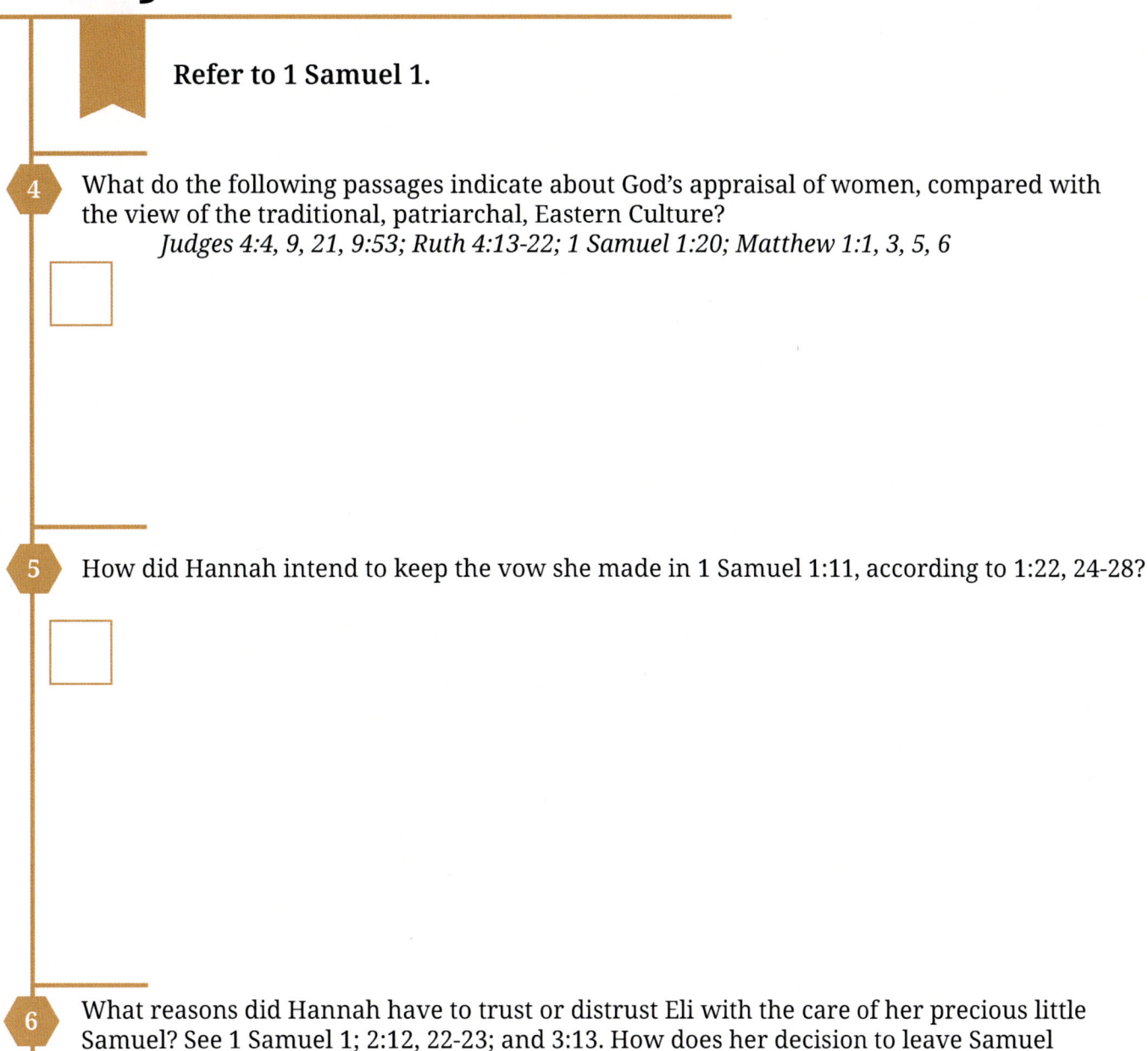

Refer to 1 Samuel 1.

4 What do the following passages indicate about God's appraisal of women, compared with the view of the traditional, patriarchal, Eastern Culture?
Judges 4:4, 9, 21, 9:53; Ruth 4:13-22; 1 Samuel 1:20; Matthew 1:1, 3, 5, 6

5 How did Hannah intend to keep the vow she made in 1 Samuel 1:11, according to 1:22, 24-28?

6 What reasons did Hannah have to trust or distrust Eli with the care of her precious little Samuel? See 1 Samuel 1; 2:12, 22-23; and 3:13. How does her decision to leave Samuel impact your thinking about a struggle or decision you face?

Day 3

📖 **Read 1 Samuel 2.**

7. Compare Hannah's prayer in 1 Samuel 2:1-10 with Mary's "song" in Luke 1:46-55. What subjects do both women address?

8. How did Eli's sons disregard the Lord in 1 Samuel 2:12-17? See Leviticus 3:16, 7:29-31.

9. Compare 1 Samuel 2:5, 20-21 with Joel 2:25a and Romans 11:35-36. Even though God owes us nothing, can you think of a time when He graciously extended special blessing to you after a season of difficulty or suffering? If so, write out your own words of praise to Him.

Day 4

Refer to 1 Samuel 2.

10 In 1 Samuel 2:12-36, the author clearly intended to sharply contrast the characters. Describe the contrasts and include verse numbers.

11 What did the Lord accuse Eli of in 1 Samuel 2:27-36, and what consequences would he suffer?

12 What promise and warning do you find in 1 Samuel 2:30, Psalm 18:25-27, and Proverbs 3:34? Name some specific ways you will plan to honor the Lord in your life this week.

Day 5

📖 **Read 1 Samuel 3.**

13 Compare 1 Samuel 3:1 with Judges 21:25 and recall the spiritually dark period in which these events took place.

14 What was located in Shiloh? This was the town where Elkanah and his family traveled annually for worship, the location where Hannah left Samuel to serve the Lord, and the place where Samuel was ministering when the Lord spoke to him. See Exodus 40:1-17, Joshua 18:1, Judges 18:31, and 1 Samuel 1:3, 24, 3:21.

15 According to 1 Samuel 3:9-10, Samuel took Eli's advice, remained where he was lying, and said, "Speak, Lord, for your servant is listening." What might be keeping you from hearing the Lord's voice today?

Prayer Requests / Additional Notes

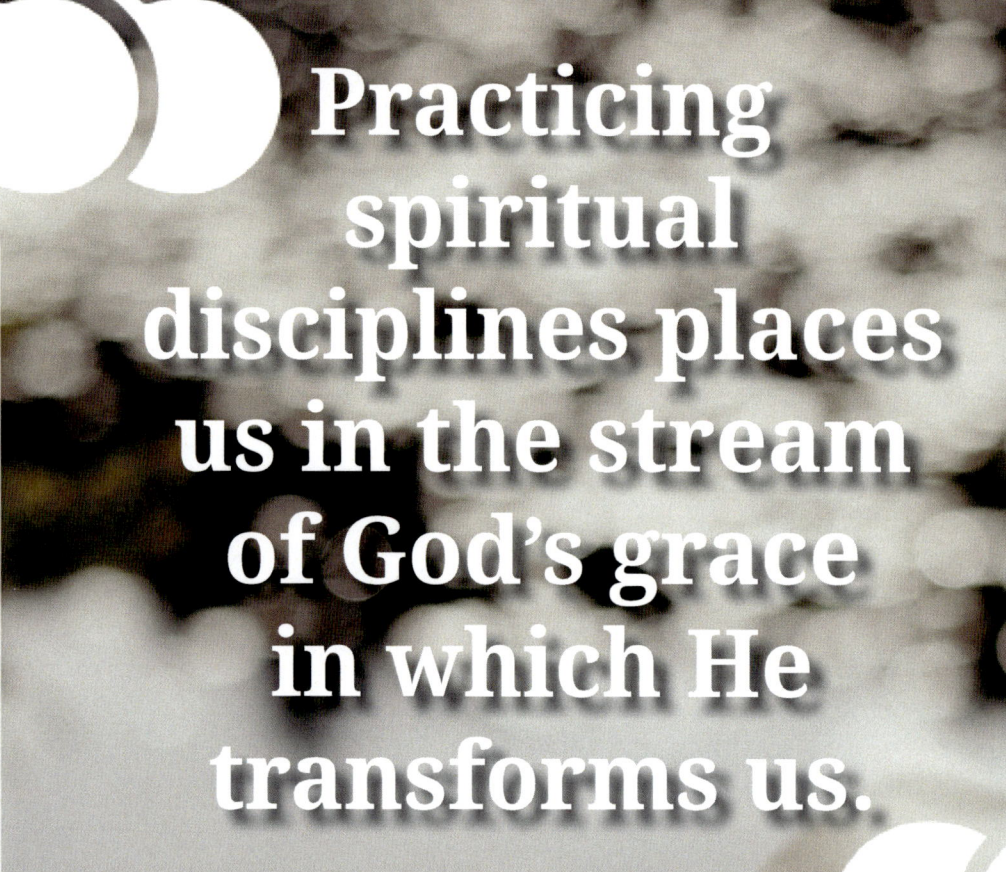

> **Practicing spiritual disciplines places us in the stream of God's grace in which He transforms us.**

Point your phone camera here to view the Lesson 7 Video.

Samuel's Birth and Call
Closing Summary of 1 Samuel 1-3

I. Hannah's Life of Prayer - 1 Samuel 1:1-2:10

Principle: True _____ is transformational.

II. Samuel's Growth Amidst Priestly Corruption - 1 Samuel 2:11-36

Principle: When combined, _____ and _____ ingrain new habits of thinking and behavior.

III. Samuel's Call - 1 Samuel 3:1-21

Principle: Inward _____ and _____ enable us to see and hear.

Lesson Eight

The Exile of the Ark and Samuel's Leadership

1 Samuel 4-7

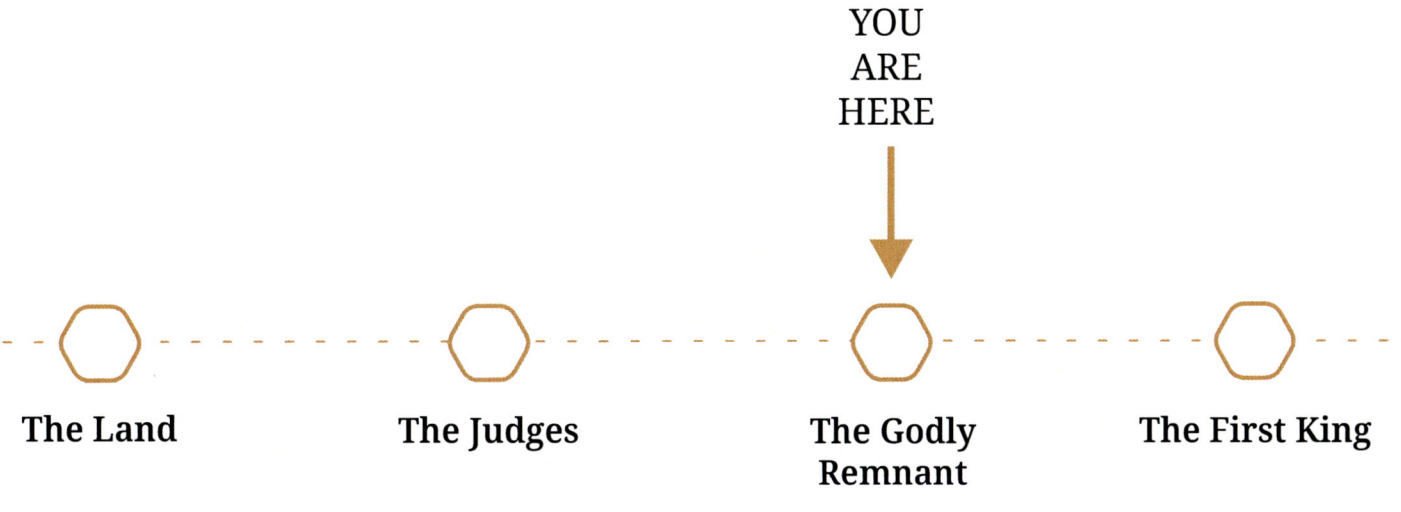

YOU ARE HERE

The Land — The Judges — The Godly Remnant — The First King

Day 1

📖 **Read 1 Samuel 4:1-11.**

1. After the Philistines defeated the Israelites in battle (1 Samuel 4:2), what did the Israelites conclude had gone wrong and why would they have come to this conclusion? Consider 1 Samuel 4:4 in light of God's words in Exodus 25:20-22, 29:42-46 and Israel's past experiences in Numbers 7:89, Joshua 6:6-11, 20-21.

2. What do we know about the spiritual condition of the Israelites in the period of the Judges that offers insight about why their solution failed? Compare Judges 2:19-22, 21:25 and 1 Samuel 3:1 with Deuteronomy 6:5 and 1 Peter 4:17.

3. Reread 1 Samuel 4:6-9. The Philistines had a confused view about the God of Israel.

⟨a⟩ How was their view a reflection of what Israel had modeled to them? Cross reference 1 Samuel 4:6-8 with Exodus 20:3-6, Judges 3:5-6, 6:24-25, 8:27, 33, 10:6, and 18:30-31.

⟨b⟩ Are you modeling anything that might leave someone confused about the God you worship? If so, what?

Day 2

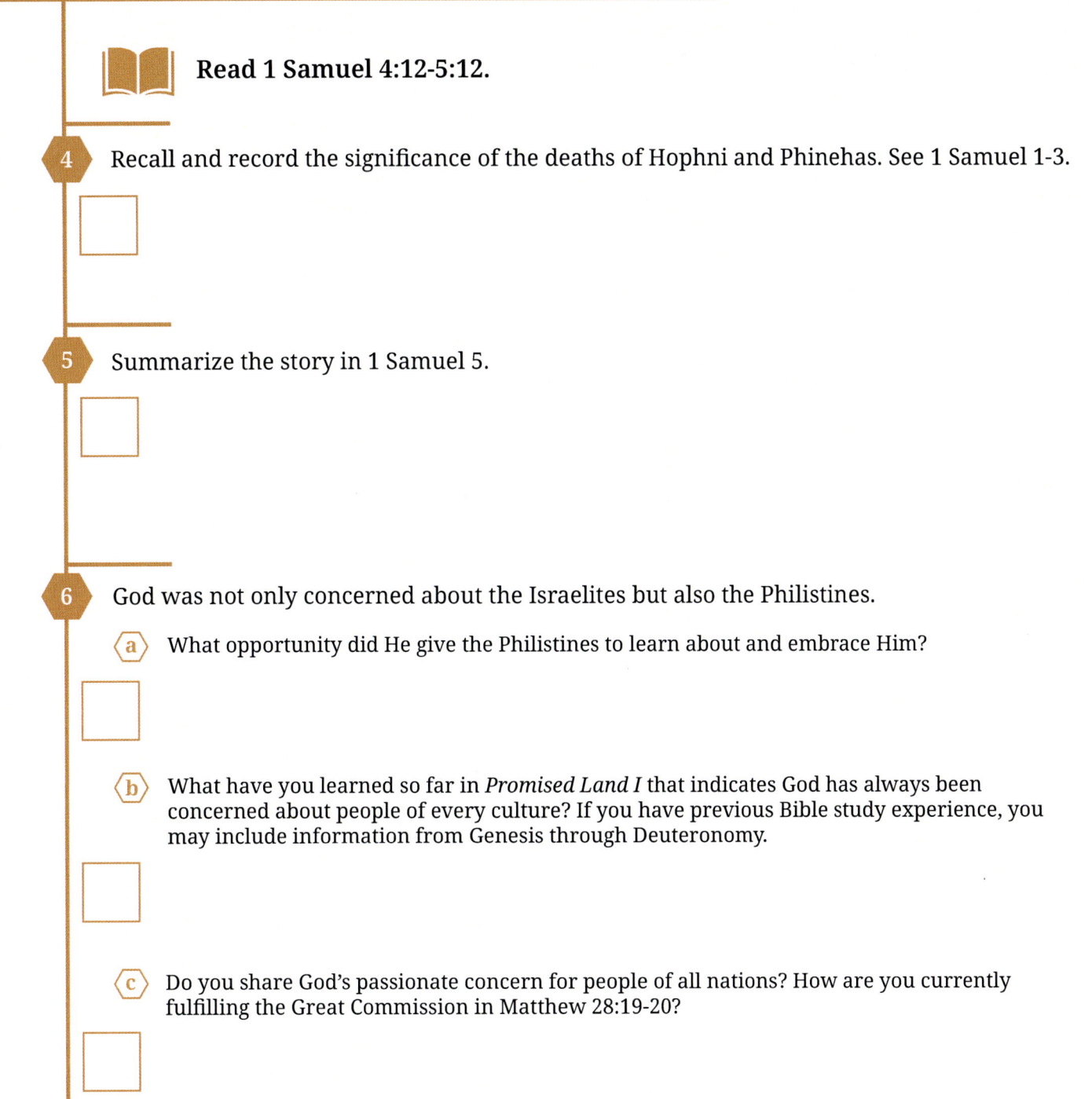

📖 **Read 1 Samuel 4:12-5:12.**

4 Recall and record the significance of the deaths of Hophni and Phinehas. See 1 Samuel 1-3.

5 Summarize the story in 1 Samuel 5.

6 God was not only concerned about the Israelites but also the Philistines.

  a What opportunity did He give the Philistines to learn about and embrace Him?

  b What have you learned so far in *Promised Land I* that indicates God has always been concerned about people of every culture? If you have previous Bible study experience, you may include information from Genesis through Deuteronomy.

  c Do you share God's passionate concern for people of all nations? How are you currently fulfilling the Great Commission in Matthew 28:19-20?

Day 3

📖 **Read 1 Samuel 6.**

7 What experiment did the Philistines conduct? Which verse summarizes it?

8 1 Samuel 6:19 tells us the Lord put to death 70 Israelites who looked into the Ark. What had they done wrong? See Numbers 4:5, 15, 20, Joshua 3:3, 1 Samuel 6:15, 2 Samuel 6:6-7, and 1 Samuel 6:20.

9 The Israelites at Beth Shemesh asked, "Who can stand in the presence of the Lord, this holy God?" (1 Samuel 6:20).

  a How did the Philistines attempt to meet God's holy standard in their own way (chapter 6)?

  b How do people today respond to the idea that God has a holy standard?

  c According to Hebrews 11:6 and 10:19-22, what is the sole basis upon which one can approach and appease a Holy God?

  d Which of your neighbors, co-workers, relatives, friends, or acquaintances is actively attempting to meet God's holy standard in their own way and needs to hear this good news?

Day 4

Read 1 Samuel 7.

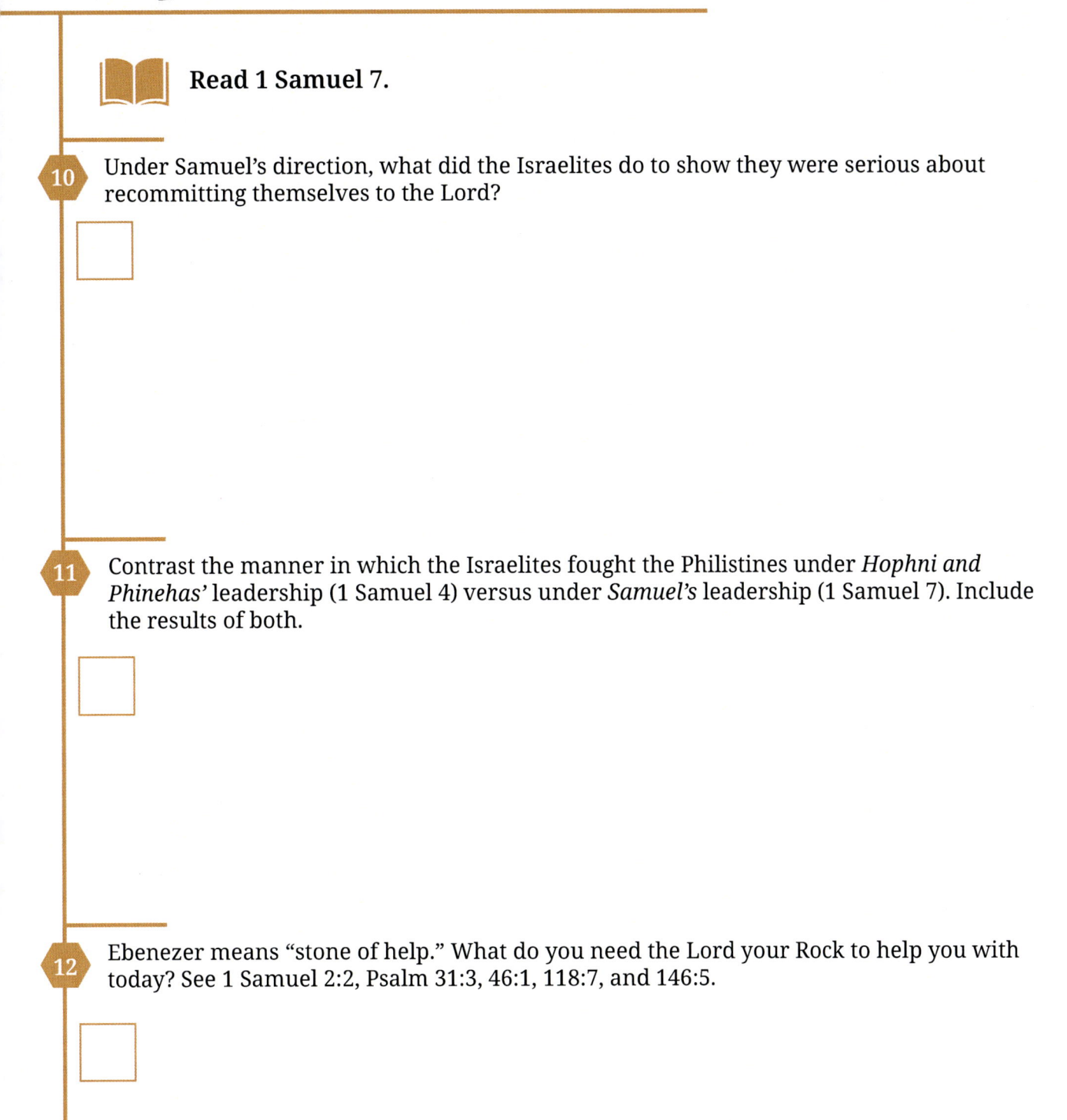

10 Under Samuel's direction, what did the Israelites do to show they were serious about recommitting themselves to the Lord?

11 Contrast the manner in which the Israelites fought the Philistines under *Hophni and Phinehas'* leadership (1 Samuel 4) versus under *Samuel's* leadership (1 Samuel 7). Include the results of both.

12 Ebenezer means "stone of help." What do you need the Lord your Rock to help you with today? See 1 Samuel 2:2, Psalm 31:3, 46:1, 118:7, and 146:5.

Day 5

📖 Read 1 Samuel 4-7.

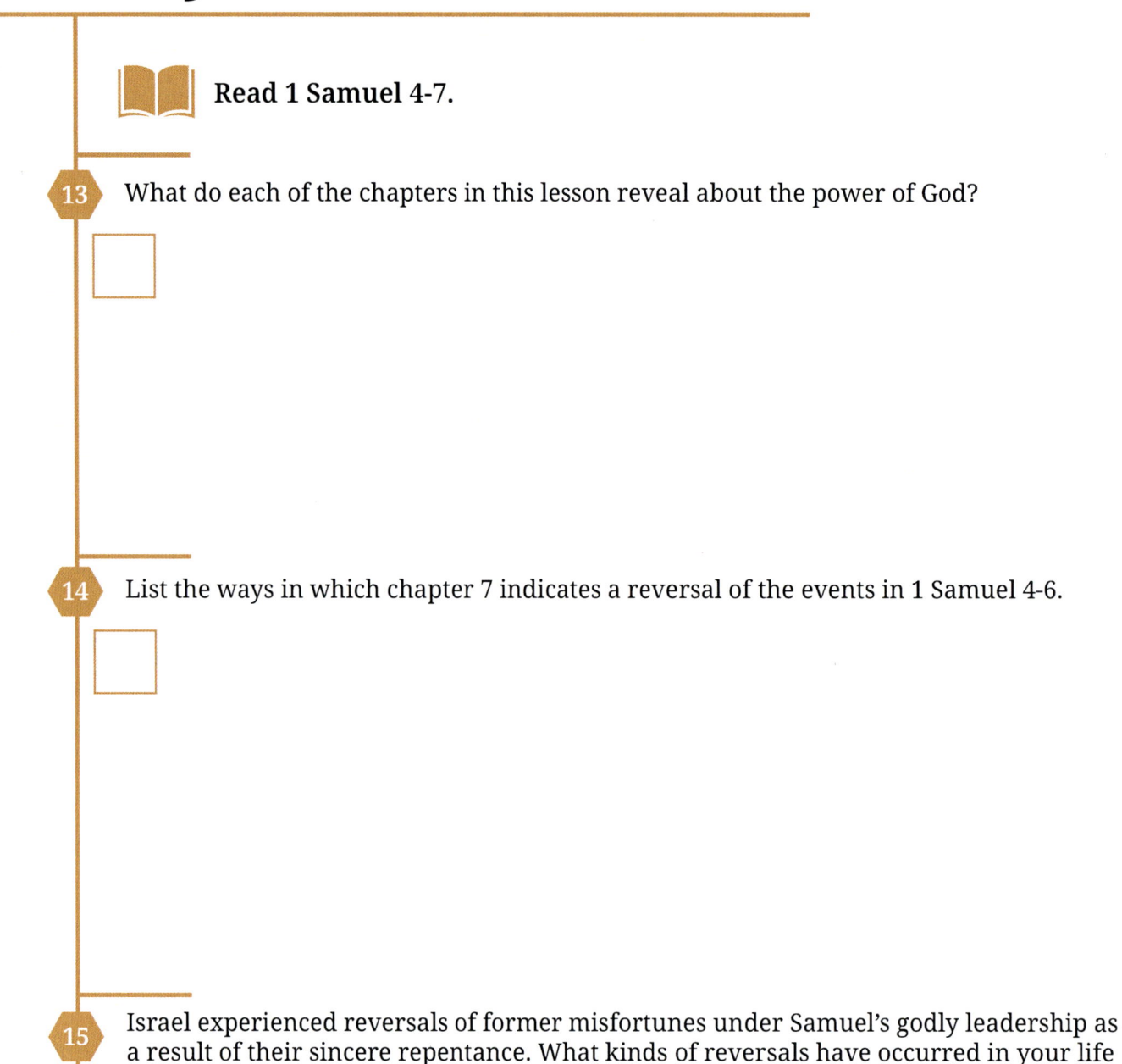

13 What do each of the chapters in this lesson reveal about the power of God?

14 List the ways in which chapter 7 indicates a reversal of the events in 1 Samuel 4-6.

15 Israel experienced reversals of former misfortunes under Samuel's godly leadership as a result of their sincere repentance. What kinds of reversals have occurred in your life since you first repented of your sins? What specific change or reversal will you ask the Almighty God to begin making within you today? See Philippians 2:12-13.

Prayer Requests / Additional Notes

> We can sometimes win physical battles in our own strength and by our own wits, but spiritual battles cannot be won this way.

Point your phone camera here to view the Lesson 8 Video.

The Exile of the Ark and Samuel's Leadership
Closing Summary of 1 Samuel 4-7

I. The Ark Captured - 1 Samuel 4

Principle: Our religious acts or relics cannot _____ _____ _____.

II. The Ark in Philistia and its Return - 1 Samuel 5-6

Principle: To accept God's omnipotence is to accept _____ _____ _____.

III. The Israelites' Victory - 1 Samuel 7

Principle: Those who _____ _____ before the Lord see His power at work on their behalf.

105

Lesson Nine

Monarchy: Saul and Samuel

1 Samuel 8-12

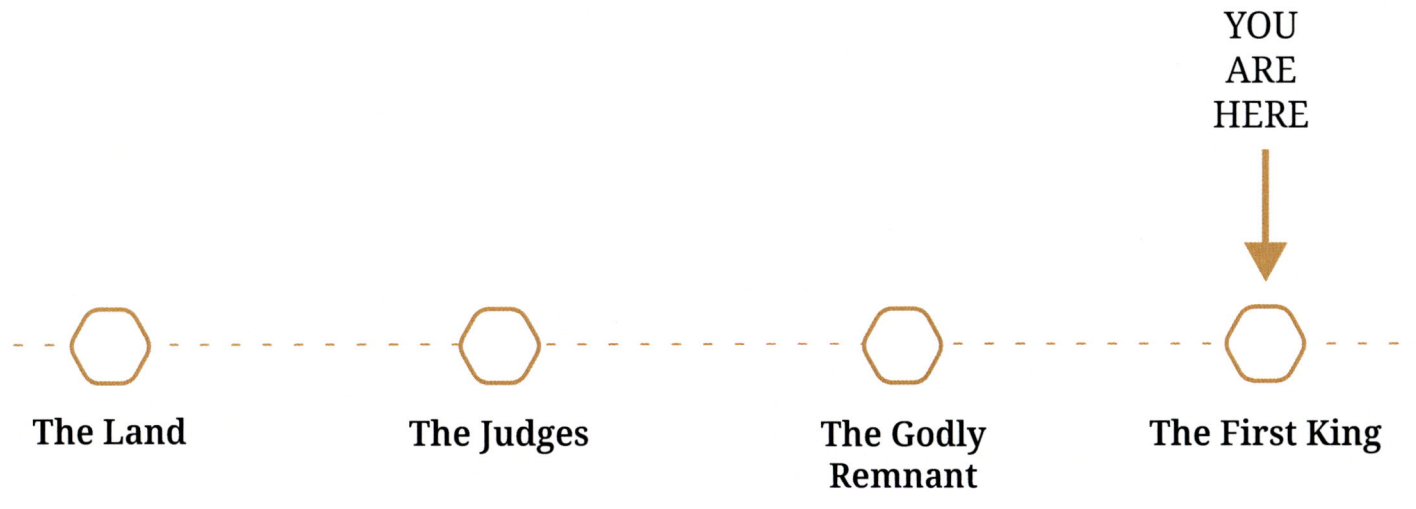

YOU ARE HERE

The Land — The Judges — The Godly Remnant — The First King

Day 1

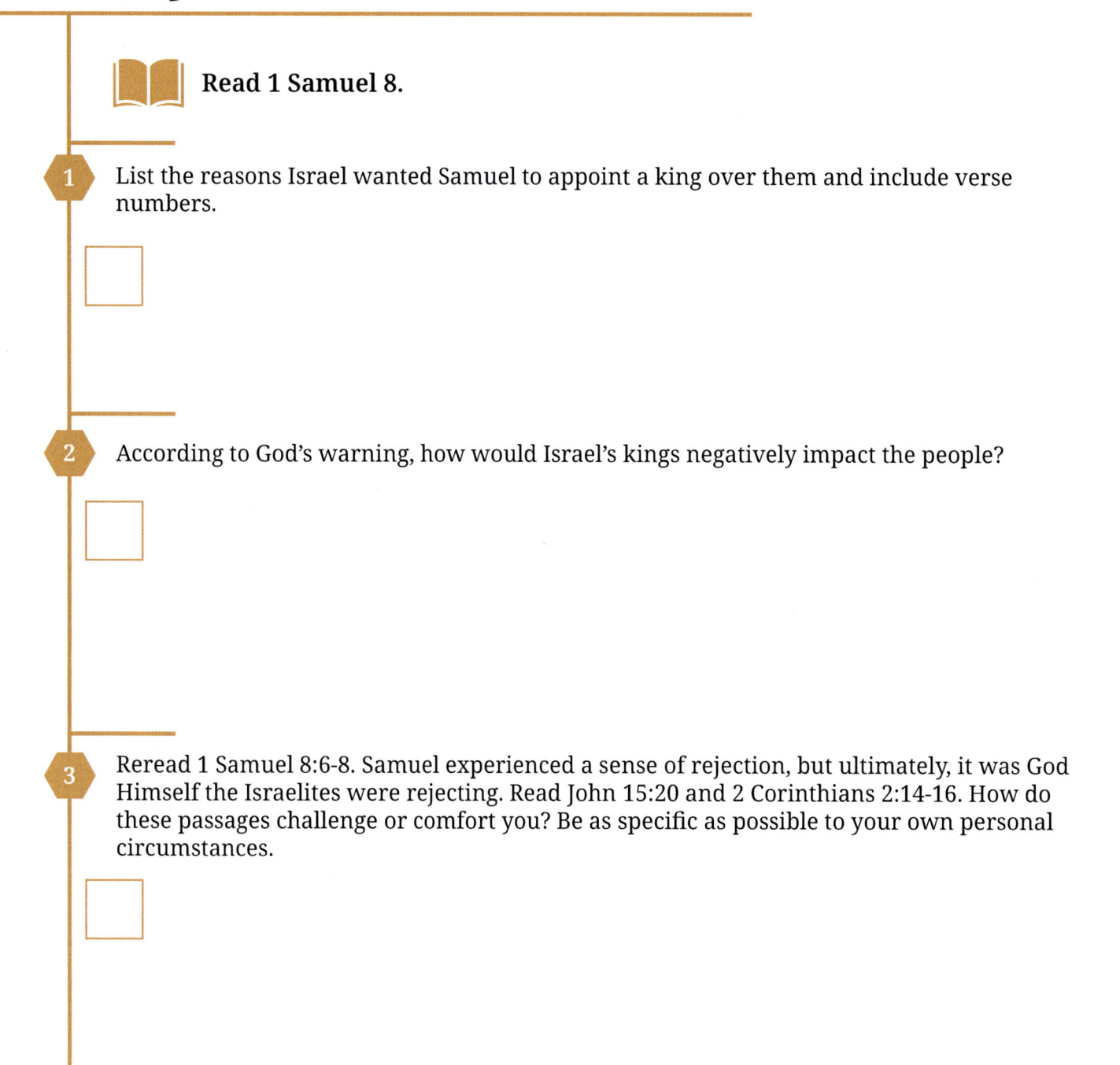

📖 **Read 1 Samuel 8.**

1 List the reasons Israel wanted Samuel to appoint a king over them and include verse numbers.

2 According to God's warning, how would Israel's kings negatively impact the people?

3 Reread 1 Samuel 8:6-8. Samuel experienced a sense of rejection, but ultimately, it was God Himself the Israelites were rejecting. Read John 15:20 and 2 Corinthians 2:14-16. How do these passages challenge or comfort you? Be as specific as possible to your own personal circumstances.

Day 2

Read 1 Samuel 9.

4. Record all you learn about Saul, his family, Samuel, and Samuel's duties from 1 Samuel 9.

5. Read Deuteronomy 18:21-22 with 1 Samuel 3:19 and 9:6. What proved that a person was a true prophet of God?

6. Reread 1 Samuel 9:14-17 with Proverbs 16:9. When Saul set out to find "the seer," he had no idea that his encounter with Samuel had been providentially arranged.
Is there a person you have recently encountered, or even someone you have known a while, who might be in your life by divine orchestration? Will you ask the Lord to put a name in your mind and begin revealing His intended purpose in the intersection of your lives? Perhaps there is something He wants you to learn from this person or some way He wants to use you in their lives.

Day 3

📖 **Read 1 Samuel 10.**

7 Reread 1 Samuel 8:22 as a reminder that Israel was waiting for Samuel to appoint a king. What indications does chapter 10 give that Saul was in no way positioning himself to become Israel's king and perhaps was even hesitant to take the role?

8 In addition to its use for fuel, cosmetic, and medicinal purposes, the Bible also speaks of oil as being used for anointing, which meant setting apart for a special purpose. 1 Samuel 10:1 says that Samuel anointed Saul with oil.

⟨a⟩ Record what you learn about anointing from the following passages:
Exodus 30:23-33; 1 Samuel 10:1, 6 and 16:13; 2 Corinthians 1:21-22; 1 John 2:20, 27.

⟨b⟩ Describe your present attitude toward a particular circumstance. Then, explain how knowing that *you* have been set apart and equipped for God's special purpose can change it.

Day 4

📖 Read 1 Samuel 11.

9 Describe the events in 1 Samuel 11 and their relationship to Saul's confirmation as king at the end of the chapter.

10 According to 1 Samuel 11:7, what was behind the Israelites' motivation to unite and defend Jabesh Gilead? Was it fear of either Saul or Samuel?

11 At this period in Israel's history, it seemed unlikely that its disconnected tribes could unite to defend one town. Is there someone you know, and need to pray for, who has a heart that seems unlikely or impossible to change?

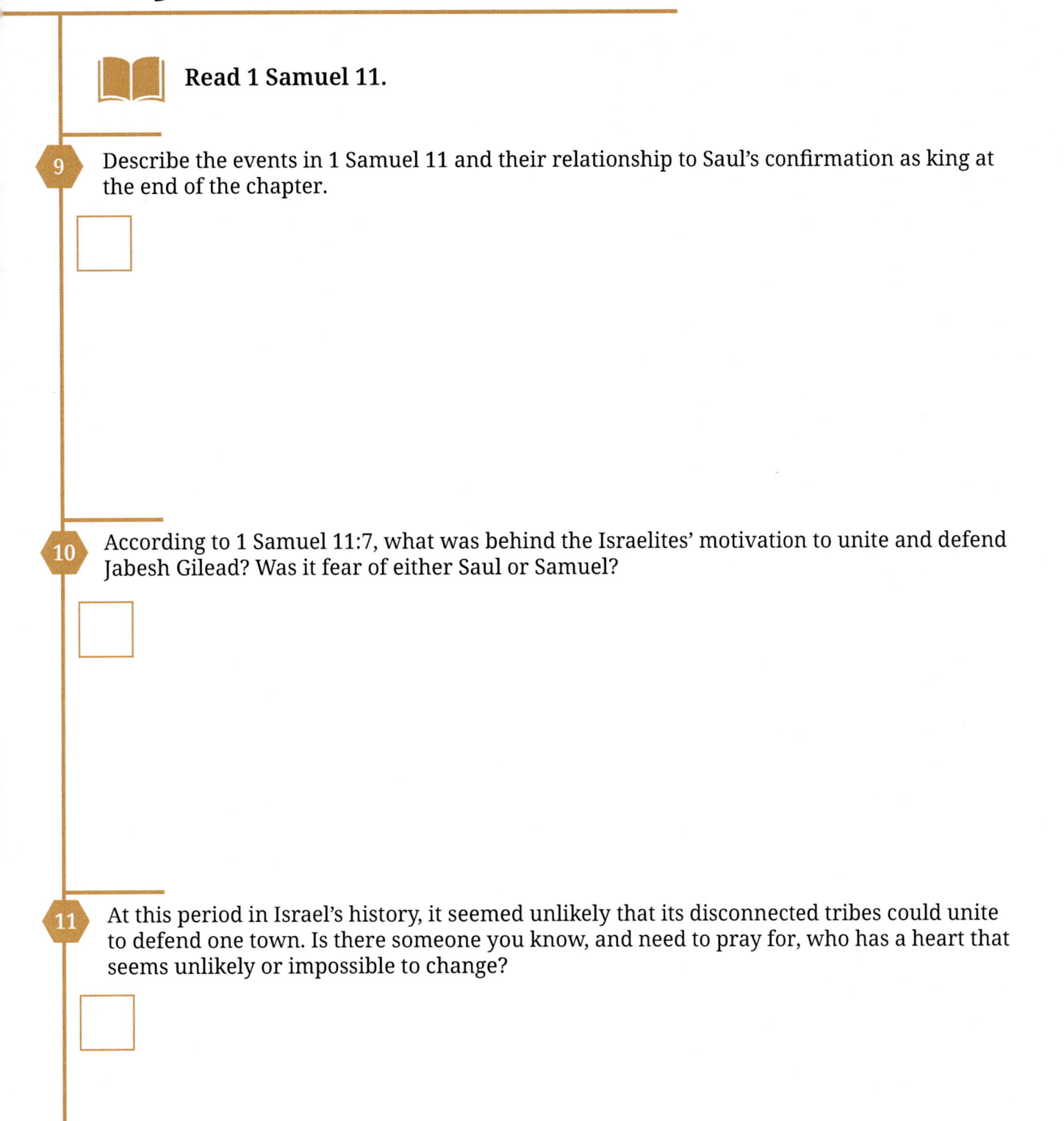

111

Day 5

📖 **Read 1 Samuel 12.**

12 Samuel began his farewell speech by reminding the Israelites that he had proven himself trustworthy (1 Samuel 12:1-5). After considering the remainder of his speech, explain why it was important for him to begin as he did.

13 Was it God's will for Israel to have a king or not? What was God's purpose with regard to kingship in Israel? Refer to Genesis 17:6 (God's promise to Abraham), Deuteronomy 17:14-20 (Moses' instructions to the Israelites just before they entered the Promised Land), and 1 Samuel 8:5-7, 10:1, 11:1 with 12:12, 14, 17, 19.

14 Based upon what you have discovered thus far in Promised Land 1, what needs in Israel did God meet by giving them their first king?

15 Examine each phrase at the close of Samuel's speech (1 Samuel 12:20-25) and list the elements of spiritual leadership Samuel modeled. Which example will you follow or which instruction will you share with someone this week?

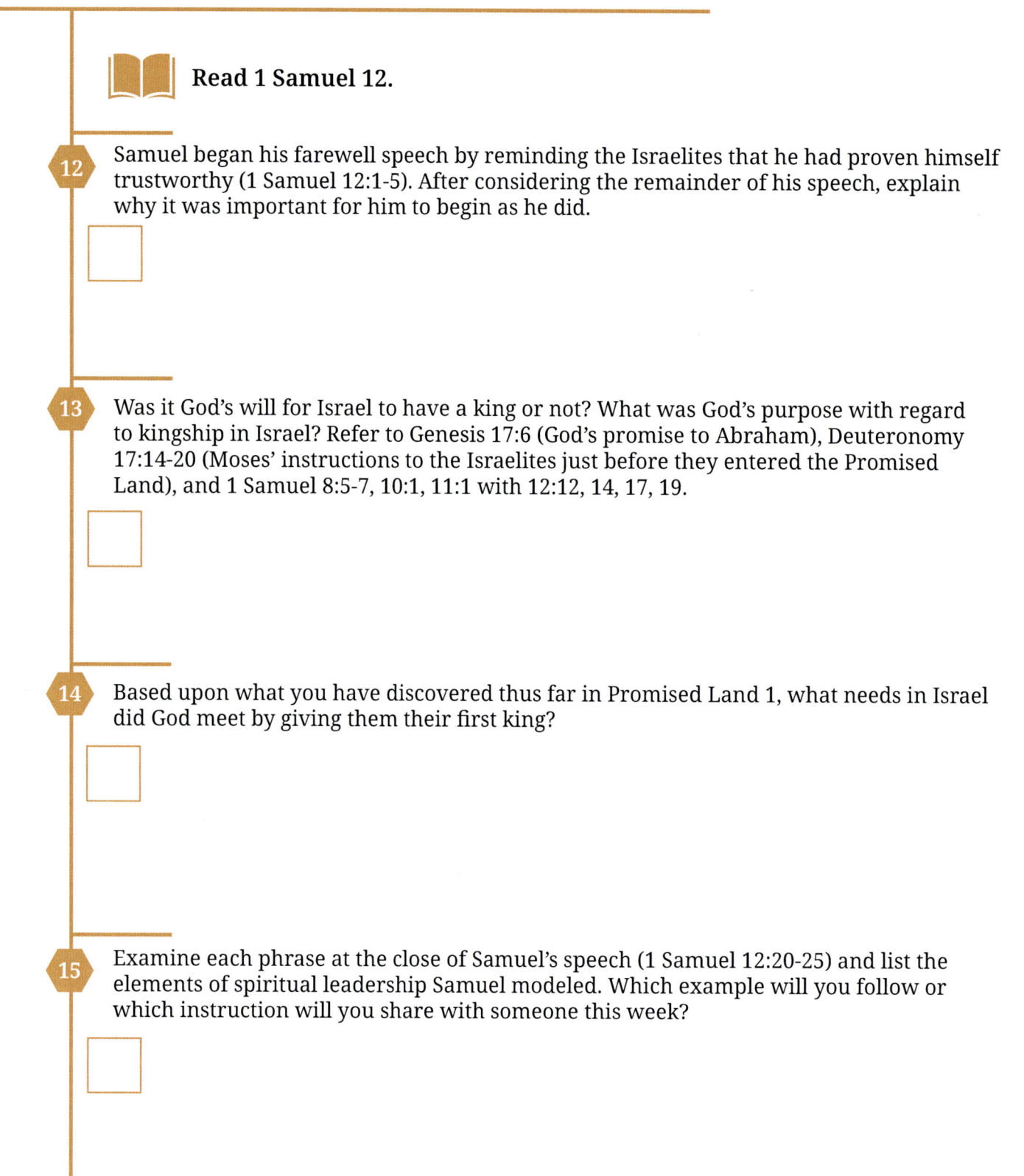

Prayer Requests / Additional Notes

> **When God is King over us, we experience true security.**

Point your phone camera here to view the Lesson 9 Video.

Monarchy: Saul and Samuel
Closing Summary of 1 Samuel 8-12

I. Israel's Request for a King - 1 Samuel 8

Principle: We should exercise caution in what we ask of the Lord, because _____ _____ _____ _____ exactly what we request.

II. Saul's Transition to Kingship - 1 Samuel 9-11

Principle: God's prescription for leadership requires _____ _____ on Him.

III. Samuel's Confrontation Over Kingship - 1 Samuel 12

Principle: Sin breeds insecurity, but _____ and _____ on the Lord's mighty works reminds us that in Him we are secure.

Lesson Ten

Looking It Over

Joshua-1 Samuel 12

- The Land
- The Judges
- The Godly Remnant
- The First King

Looking It Over

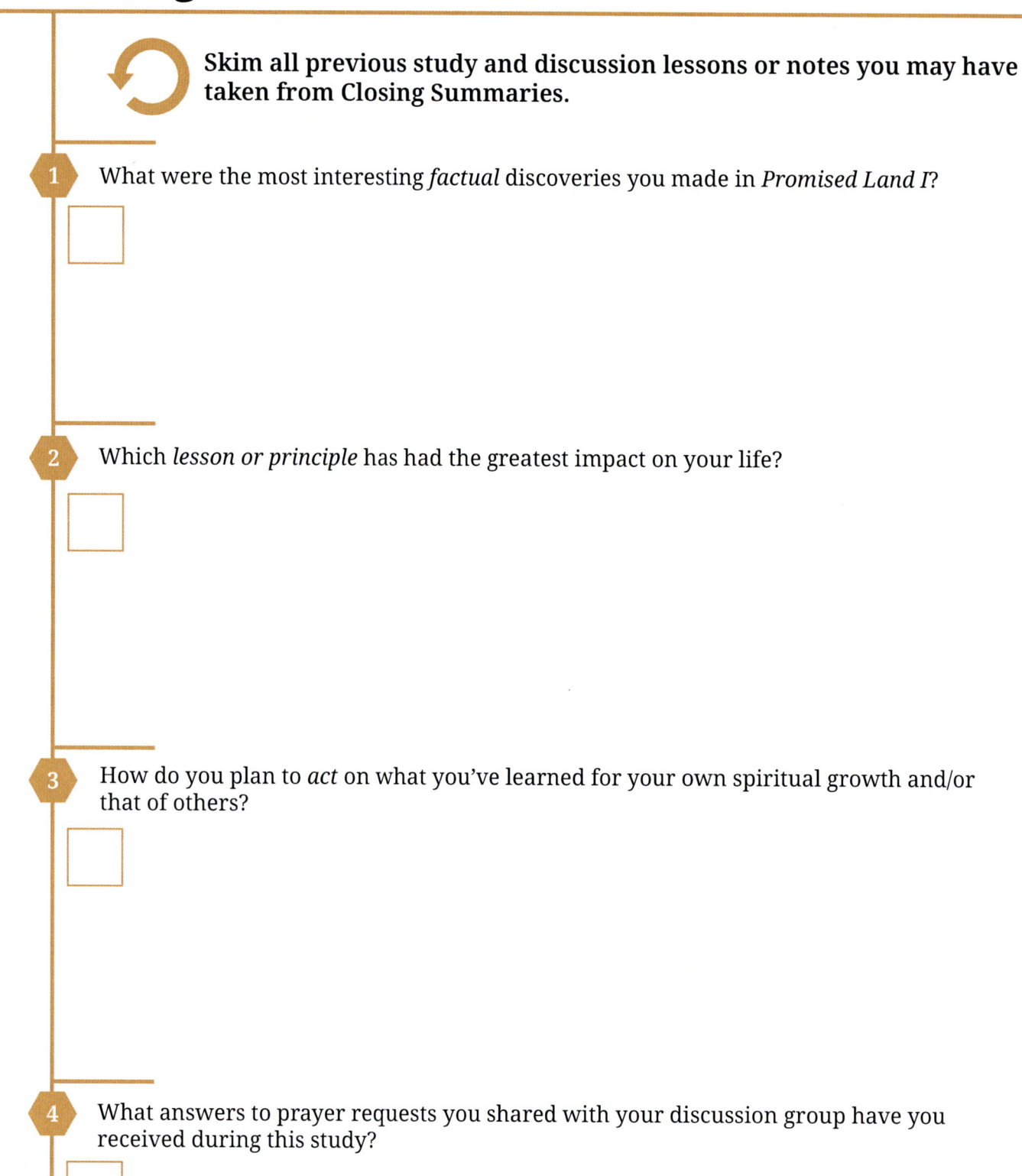

Skim all previous study and discussion lessons or notes you may have taken from Closing Summaries.

1 What were the most interesting *factual* discoveries you made in *Promised Land I*?

2 Which *lesson or principle* has had the greatest impact on your life?

3 How do you plan to *act* on what you've learned for your own spiritual growth and/or that of others?

4 What answers to prayer requests you shared with your discussion group have you received during this study?

Prayer Requests / Additional Notes

"God has proven His **faithfulness** to His **promises** and His **people**."

Point your phone camera here to view the Lesson 10 Video.

Looking it Over
Closing Summary of Joshua-1 Samuel 12

I. The Conquest of Canaan - Book of Joshua

Principle: God is faithful to all His _____.

II. The Leadership of the Judges - Judges, Ruth, 1 Samuel 1-12

Principle: God is faithful to His _____, even when they are not faithful to Him.

MATTHEW 9:3

LEADER'S MANUAL

Leading a Discussion

I. YOUR INITIAL SMALL GROUP MEETING

Ideally, you will meet once with your group *before* working on your first lesson. Page 13 has a rough schedule for this initial meeting.

ESTABLISH GROUP EXPECTATIONS

People are likely to come to your group with very different ideas about what happens in a small group. Setting group expectations is one of the major goals of this meeting. Group members need to know what they can expect from the GOTW study, what they can expect from you, and what you expect of them. Setting group expectations *in the beginning* prevents confusion and also helps avoid complications that can arise in group discussion. With this in mind, use a portion of your initial meeting to review the weekly structure of your meetings and the instructions on pages 13 through 15. These instructions were designed to explain the GOTW method of study and establish expectations that foster healthy group dynamics.

Please be positive in your presentation, avoiding negative, rule-making language (*"Don't do this,"* or *"Make sure you do that"* or *"You must do such-and-such"*). Instead, emphasize the ways in which the instructions benefit each individual in the group and the group as a whole. Should certain difficulties later occur within the group, having previously read and agreed upon these gives you a basis upon which to address them ("Remember when we talked about...?").

WATCH THE INTRODUCTORY VIDEO

Each GOTW Bible study has a unique introductory video that overviews the subject, explains where the covered material falls within the story of the Bible, and in some cases, includes other general Bible information. For this reason, it is intended to be watched in your initial meeting, before the group begins work on their first lesson. Hopefully, the video will help generate enthusiasm within the group for studying the particular part of the Bible covered by the study. A content outline is included for note-taking. The QR code and outline for the introductory video can be found on pages 20 and 21.

II. ADVANCE PREPARATION

Prior preparation is the key to successfully facilitating a discussion.

COMPLETE YOUR OWN LESSON

It's important for your own spiritual growth, and for the sake of good discussion-leading, that you complete your lesson independently without consulting the answers in the leaders' guide, notes in Study Bibles, or other commentaries. We cannot lead others where we haven't been ourselves.

UNDERLINE THE KEY WORD OR PHRASE

While completing your own lesson, underline the key word or phrase in each question. For what does the question ask? A name, a verse number, an opinion, a phrase, a list, etc. Later, if you get distracted during the discussion, you'll be able to recall the gist of the question at a glance and bring the group back on track.

READ THE ANSWERS IN THE LEADERS' GUIDE

Once you've finished your lesson, read the answers in the leaders' guide to ensure you properly understood each question. In many cases, the printed answers are not comprehensive. On other occasions, they include more information than you should expect to hear from your group. Please don't check your group's answers for accuracy by comparing them with the answers in the leaders' guide during your discussion. That level of scrutiny will not result in relaxed and enjoyable sharing. The given answers are also not intended to be shared by you with your group. The videos usually contain a good bit of that information.

PLEASE NOTE: No answers are provided for the final review lesson entitled, "Looking It Over." On that particular week, the lesson only contains four questions, all of which are personal in nature.

PRAY, PRAY, PRAY

Personal prayer for your individual group members and your weekly time together is an all-important step in preparing to lead!

II. ADVANCE PREPARATION CONT.

PLAN THE TIMING OF THE DISCUSSION

You might have real doubts about whether it's important to keep track of the time when discussing something as important as God's word. Well, *it is* for several reasons. First, someone in your group may have an appointment to keep, a babysitter to bring home, or if you're meeting in the evening, an early wake-up time the following day. If you repeatedly exceed your planned ending time, those people will simply stop coming. Secondly, your group is likely to be silently frustrated if you fail to discuss all fifteen questions each week. Invariably, someone's favorite will be one of the last. Additionally, you have probably presented the study as an 11, 12, 13, or 14-week study. If you carry over questions from week to week, you won't be able to keep what your group perceives as a commitment to finish the study by a certain date. On the other hand, both you and your group will be frustrated if you're constantly looking at the clock as you lead. You do not want to give the impression that you're not listening attentively. *The key is creating a time-guide* for your eyes only--one that will help you move the group through the entire lesson in the allotted time while allowing some flexibility. Without this tool, you'll inevitably run out of time or end too quickly.

Write your planned starting time at the beginning of your lesson and your scheduled ending time after the last question. The recommended amount of time for group discussion of a GOTW lesson is 40 minutes. Next, decide upon an approximate number of minutes to spend on each question. Thirty seconds per individual answer is a good estimate. Obviously, some people and questions will take much longer to answer and some much less. As a guide to determining how much time to spend discussing each question, consider the nature of the question.

Level 1 ("Open and Shut") Questions

These questions have a clear and succinct answer that's easily seen in the Bible text. If the question asks for the name of Jesus' mother, obviously, the only answer is, "Mary." These questions need little time, probably one minute at most. Allow one person to give the answer and immediately move on. Asking, "Does anyone have anything to add?" only confuses the group and wastes time. Contrary to the example above, many "open and shut" questions do not have answers that the average person knows without consulting the text. It is important for *you* to know what the correct answer is so you don't move on until it is given. Reviewing the printed answers prior to leading will help you avoid this mistake.

Level 2 Questions

These questions require more thought and research within the Bible text than a Level 1 question. The time you allow for these will vary. Gauge the degree of enrichment it will bring to the spiritual lives of those in your group. Questions that lead to the clarification of Bible doctrines are critical to spiritual growth, while questions that ask for personal opinions or speculation have far less value, even though they may be fun to discuss. Some questions will also simply take longer to answer than others. You might plan for two or three people to answer a Level 2 question (1-2 minutes), and on some occasions, you might expect five or more people to answer (2-4 minutes).

Level 3 (Personal Application) Questions

Discussion facilitators are accountable to the Lord to encourage group members to *apply* what they are learning, both by your own example--sharing your personal and specific answer to an application question, from time to time--and by regularly reminding the group that *life change* is the ultimate goal of discipleship. Each lesson generally has five personal application questions, one per day. Ideally, the most amount of time should be devoted to discussing these. Again, the time will vary depending on the particular question. Although discussion leaders are not generally encouraged to share their answers, i.e., teach, personal application questions are an important exception.

Write an estimated number of minutes to spend in discussion next to each question. Next, add up all your estimated minutes. If they exceed 40, reduce the minutes given to questions with less spiritual value *and plan to move the group on, if needed, with the explanation that you want to make sure they have time to talk about all fifteen questions.* If your minutes total less than 40, add time to the questions your group will most benefit from discussing.

Once you've made all necessary adjustments and your minutes total 40, write specific clock times next to each question. Hopefully, you will be very interested and engaged in listening to your group's answers. For this reason, you're not likely to notice the time before or after discussing every single question. Yet, by having a clock time next to *each one*, you'll have confidence that at any given point in the discussion you can see, at a glance, whether you're relatively on time or running behind.

Learning how to balance good stewardship of time with genuine interest in those in your group is critical. If your temperament is task-oriented, monitoring the time or checking answers for completeness can take too high of a priority. On the other hand, if you are people-oriented, time may easily escape you. Ask the Lord to develop you into a well-balanced leader.

See annotated example on next page →

Leader Example

Write your opening statement here

KEEP IN MIND

Level 1 Questions

"Open and Shut"; only one correct answer found in the text, 1 min. max.

Level 2 Questions

Require room for thought and research within the Bible, 1-4 min.

Level 3 Questions

Personal application; sharing from multiple people, allow the most time

Annotate

Write how many people will answer and how long each question will take in the following format:

estimated number of people answering / estimated time

Maximum Time

The small group discussion should only last 40 minutes!

Starting time

2 people / 1 min.

1 person / 1 min.

3 people / 2 min.

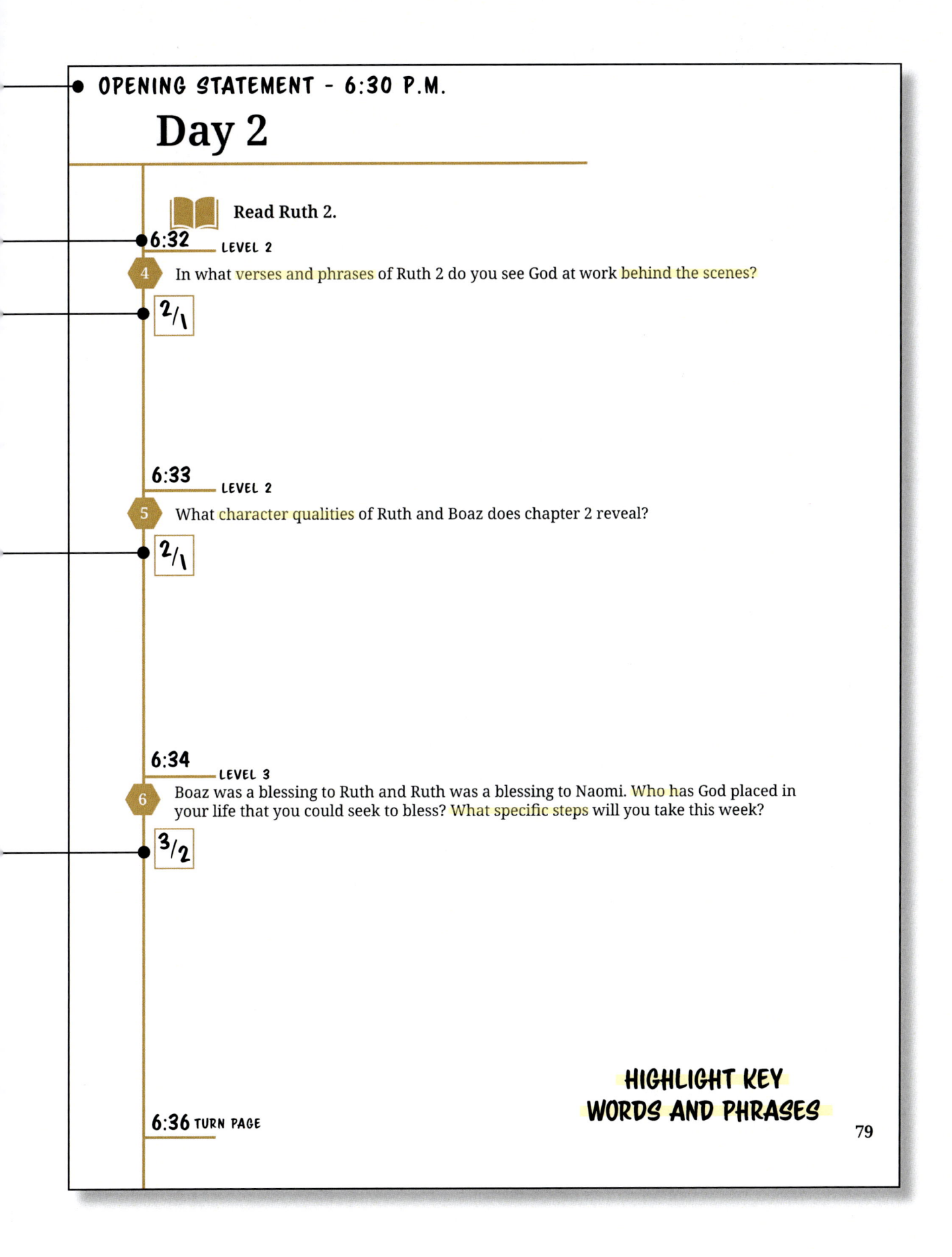

● OPENING STATEMENT - 6:30 P.M.

Day 2

📖 Read Ruth 2.

6:32 — LEVEL 2

4 In what verses and phrases of Ruth 2 do you see God at work behind the scenes?

2/1

6:33 — LEVEL 2

5 What character qualities of Ruth and Boaz does chapter 2 reveal?

2/1

6:34 — LEVEL 3

6 Boaz was a blessing to Ruth and Ruth was a blessing to Naomi. Who has God placed in your life that you could seek to bless? What specific steps will you take this week?

3/2

HIGHLIGHT KEY WORDS AND PHRASES

6:36 TURN PAGE

III. BEGINNING THE DISCUSSION

TONE

Begin every meeting by welcoming your group warmly. Use good eye contact and smile. You set the tone for the group. If you speak very quietly, they will also. If you act disinterested or bring too little energy to the group, they will become bored. If you interrupt others, so will they.

OPENING STATEMENT

Take less than a minute to give an opening statement. Beginning with a "thank you" or an encouraging word about having experienced rich sharing the previous week, great attendance, and so forth will have a very positive influence in the group. Your opening statement is not a time to give devotional thoughts, readings, interesting news items, and quotes from sermons or radio teachers. On the week that you discuss the first lesson, the group will benefit from a clarification of your role. See Paragraph 1 of Section IV for more about this aspect of your role:

> *"My role is to facilitate group discussion by ensuring we have an interesting, informative, and lively discussion. Since the purpose of this time is group sharing and discussion, I won't be directly answering the questions for you. The teaching will occur in the videos."*

Every week or two, use this time to give a very brief reminder of one of your goals or expectations (p. 14-15, 124). Most of your group will immediately recognize the benefits of the instructions and happily comply, but for a few, the methods and approach will be new and challenging. Occasionally, you may also have a group member with emotional needs that strain or hinder healthy group dynamics. For these reasons, you will do the entire group a great service by reviewing one of the agreed upon expectations in your opening statement every week or two. The idea is to try to head off difficulties before they develop. If a particular problem does occur, review the expectation that addresses it in your opening statement the very next week. Again, be positive, focusing on the benefits, but also be clear. For example, you might say,

> *"Just a quick reminder that we are aiming for a well-balanced discussion. So, if you've had one or two opportunities to share your answers, please allow others the same opportunity before giving additional input."*

On another occasion, you might remind them of a goal. This reminder is especially helpful if someone has been resisting your attempts to move the group on from question to question.

> *"Our goal is to have an interesting discussion and hear some ideas that get us thinking, not necessarily to exhaust everything that can be said about each question. In order for us to get through all fifteen of them, from time to time, I may need to move us on when we could easily share more."*

After you've given an opening word of appreciation or reminder, ask the group members to pull out their lessons and open their Bibles to the appropriate place.

IV. LEADING THE DISCUSSION

KEEP THE FOCUS ON THE GROUP

Your role as a discussion leader is to serve others. Read the questions aloud, inform the group when it is time to move to the next question, and give a brief encouragement or acknowledgment to those who share. Other than that, talk as little as possible during the discussion. This can be difficult for extroverted discussion leaders or those with teaching gifts, but the moment your group starts to believe that you will eventually give "the answer," sharing their own thoughts and discoveries will seem unnecessary and they'll be less and less willing to participate. The closing summary video contains the teaching. In addition to promoting servant leadership, this approach makes it possible for individuals to lead a Bible study without fear over the amount of Bible knowledge they bring to the table.

BODY LANGUAGE IS IMPORTANT

Smile when you talk. Turn your body toward the person talking. Ideally, your legs and arms should be uncrossed (an "open" posture). Give eye contact and show you are following what is being said with facial expressions (nodding, smiles, raised eyebrows, etc.). If your group meets virtually, your smile is especially important.

READING THE QUESTIONS

Read each question *number*, along with the question, so that people who have gotten distracted or lost their place in the lesson can quickly find it. Since it is boring for the group to listen to you read long lists of Scripture references that sometimes appear within the questions, shorten the question by substituting a phrase like, *"from the listed passages"* or *"in the verses from Deuteronomy, Romans and Revelation,"* skipping all the reference numbers.

LATECOMERS

When members arrive late, as they sometimes do, briefly welcome them and identify the number of the question currently being discussed: *"Hi Hannah! Good to see you. We're on question 4."* Then, immediately return to the group discussion: *"I'd love to hear a couple more of you respond, before we move on."*

DISCUSSION LEADING STRATEGIES
(see also Addressing Challenges on p. 136)

After reading the question, allow some silence, but if too much time passes and no one has volunteered an answer, call on someone, particularly individuals who haven't yet shared anything. From time to time, call on individuals by name just to keep everyone alert and the discussion from dragging. However, if you do this for every question, the discussion will feel too controlled. On a rare occasion, if the group remains silent, it may be necessary to say, *"Well, if no one has anything to share then we will move on."* Usually, upon hearing this, someone will be prompted to speak. If not, follow through and move on. However, you shouldn't do this regularly.

Be gracious but clear that you plan to stick with discussing the printed questions. They are certainly not the only good questions that can be asked about the Bible passages in the lesson. However, they are the questions your group has pondered prior to your meeting. The moment you begin interjecting additional questions to those on the printed material, your group will start doing the same. Although many "think tanks" operate successfully this way, it is the sound advice of experienced Bible study leaders *not* to lead your Bible study in such a fashion. In addition to a host of other problems, the group will be frustrated that they have prepared answers to questions that you will not end up having time to discuss. This causes them to lose motivation to prepare their lessons in the future. Allowing for interjection of additional questions also alienates some of the group, since one or two deep thinkers or especially talkative folks usually end up dominating the discussion.

If everyone seems confused about a question, try rereading it, emphasizing the key words. If you are sure the group understands the question yet there is still confusion or uncertainty, suggest they listen for the answer in the closing summary video.

If there is no immediate response by anyone in the group to a life-application question, be prepared to share your own personal application. Doing this from time to time will allow the group to get to know you better. It is also an opportunity for you to model *appropriate, current,* and *personal* sharing. This is an important exception to the recommendation that the discussion leader does not answer the questions.

Be prepared to graciously but firmly move the group on...

- if someone "corners" another class member by asking them to answer a question they pose, or tries to give them advice
- when someone's sharing leads the group off on a secondary subject
- when you have exhausted the time planned for that question (*"This sharing has been great, but if we don't move on, we might not get to the last question, which could have been the most important for one of us this week."*)
- when someone's sharing is inappropriate (see Addressing Challenges in your Group p. 137).

RESPONDING TO ANSWERS

The group will not know how to interpret your silence if you say nothing after someone shares an answer. The key to responding appropriately is careful listening to what each individual says. When you respond, address the individual by name. Give them eye contact, a smile, and a very brief phrase or sentence of acknowledgement, such as, "You obviously read the text very closely," "Good insight" or "That is interesting." Sometimes, a nod or a simple, *"Thank you, [name],"* is sufficient.

The counseling technique in which you repeat or rephrase a person's response back to them is not beneficial in small group Bible study discussion. It may cause the individual to feel they are unable to communicate clearly enough to bother sharing in the future. Occasionally, however, someone may have misspoken and you might need to ask for clarification so that the group isn't left confused.

When someone gives a questionable or unscriptural answer, ask for the Scripture reference or Bible translation the individual used to get their answer. Thank the person for their response and then call on someone you believe has a better grasp on the teachings of the Bible. For example, "That's interesting, Steve. Kate, how did you answer this question?" *Calling upon someone in the group whose answers tend to be reliable ensures the group isn't left with a misunderstanding, while protecting you from falling into the habit of providing answers.* If the entire group is missing the mark, wrap up the discussion on that question by suggesting that the video may provide further clarification. *"Let's listen for more about this in the video."* Then, move on.

V. LEADING PRAYER TIME

Nothing bonds a group like sharing personal prayer requests and praying together. Even more importantly, answered prayer builds faith and gives the group an opportunity to praise God! After your discussion, spend about fifteen minutes in group prayer. This is likely to be plenty of time, since much sharing has already occurred in the discussion.

Think in advance about a method of sharing and praying over requests. If you meet in the evening, keep in mind that people may be too sleepy for you to ask them to pray silently. Your prayer time needs to be natural but still controlled enough to ensure you end on time. In the first week or two, you might take requests for about ten minutes and then pray aloud for all of them yourself. As the group gets to know one another, you might ask for a volunteer to pray over each request immediately after it is given.

It is recommended that prayer requests be limited to those asked *for oneself.* Of course, you'll first need to explain this to your group. Although there are many worthwhile things to pray about, the group members are probably eager to get to know one another better, and this will help them do so. However, not everyone in your group is likely to feel comfortable sharing prayer requests *or* praying aloud. For this reason, it is best to make the giving of prayer requests and praying aloud voluntary. You can encourage participation in those who are timid by sharing your own personal requests and keeping your prayers short and free from flowery prayer language.

V. PRACTICING BALANCED LEADERSHIP

Ask the Lord to give you *gracious authority.* It takes grace *and* courage to be a good leader. Sometimes leading well means you must confront an individual who refuses to follow courteous guidelines. If you fail to address problems, you have let down the rest of the group. Group members will be silently frustrated and eventually, may not return. On the other hand, a group will also be frustrated if they feel the leader is too controlling.

SHOW GRACE BY

- allowing some silence and pauses, without wasting too much time
- smiling, giving eye contact, and loving, meaningful responses or a nod after someone has shared
- resisting the temptation to be the center of attention; giving short, affirming responses without repeating back everything a person says or asking unexpected personal questions
- working at creating a relaxed atmosphere in the group, not a rigid one

ASSUME RESPONSIBILITY BY

- kindly refusing to allow a group member to usurp your role. Allowing someone else to steer the conversation will confuse and frustrate the group. Pray God will give you confidence to do the job He has given you.
- not allowing one individual to continually dominate the discussion
- telling the group when it is time to move on
- calling on people to share, as needed
- keeping your group on the subject
- seeking assistance from experienced leaders in handling sticky situations

Your own temperament will probably cause you to naturally tend toward being a bit of a "drill sergeant" (an autocratic, dictatorial, controlling leader) or a leader who is easily overrun by others (a passive, "too soft" leader). Know yourself and work toward the middle ground – that place where you exert gracious but definite leadership. When your leadership style is well balanced, your group will feel relaxed and more eager to share.

A WORD OF ENCOURAGEMENT

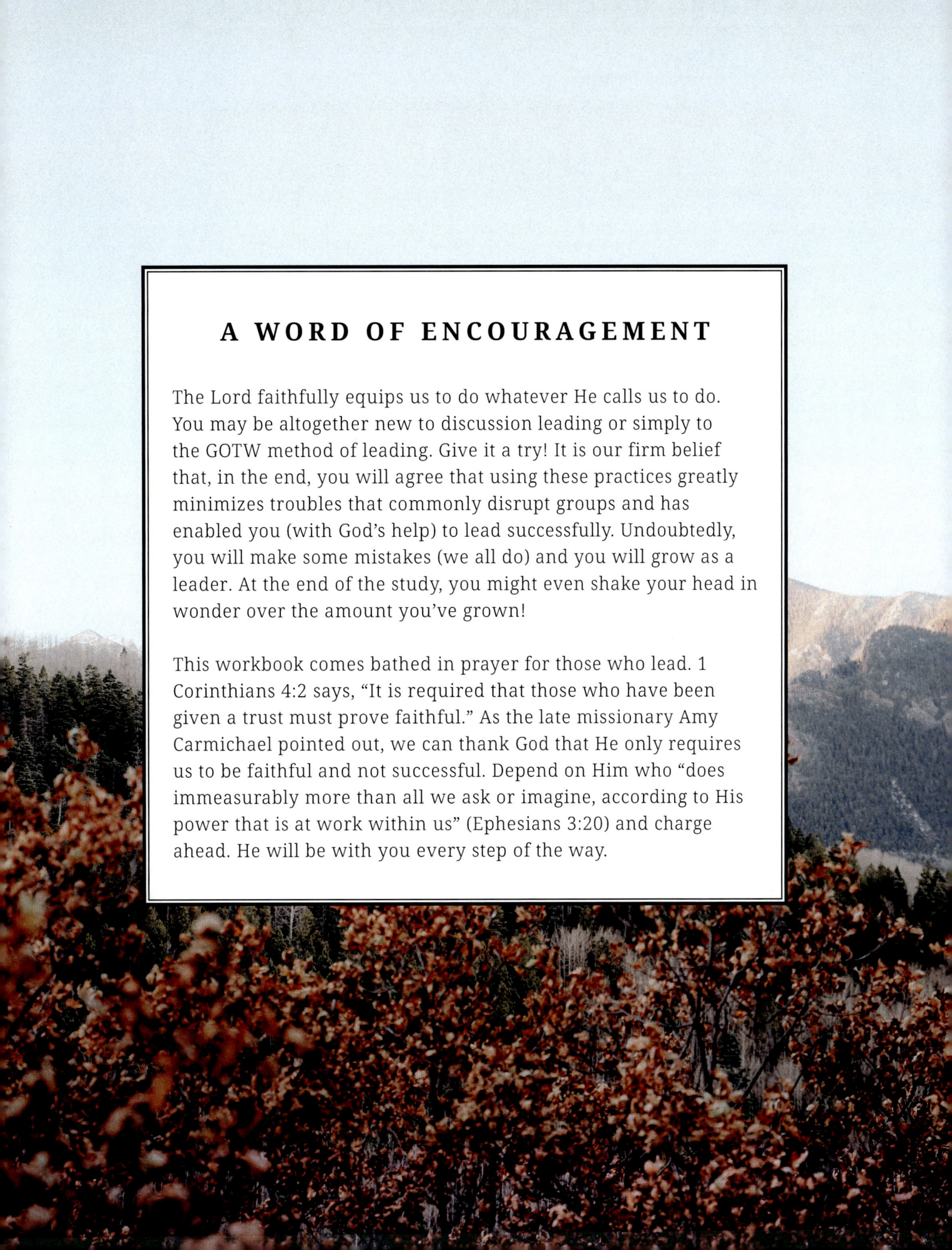

The Lord faithfully equips us to do whatever He calls us to do. You may be altogether new to discussion leading or simply to the GOTW method of leading. Give it a try! It is our firm belief that, in the end, you will agree that using these practices greatly minimizes troubles that commonly disrupt groups and has enabled you (with God's help) to lead successfully. Undoubtedly, you will make some mistakes (we all do) and you will grow as a leader. At the end of the study, you might even shake your head in wonder over the amount you've grown!

This workbook comes bathed in prayer for those who lead. 1 Corinthians 4:2 says, "It is required that those who have been given a trust must prove faithful." As the late missionary Amy Carmichael pointed out, we can thank God that He only requires us to be faithful and not successful. Depend on Him who "does immeasurably more than all we ask or imagine, according to His power that is at work within us" (Ephesians 3:20) and charge ahead. He will be with you every step of the way.

Addressing Challenges in Your Group

MEDIATING ANSWERS

Someone shares an answer that also answers the next question in full or in part.

> ▸ Accept the answer without mentioning that it is out of order. If you've already discussed the current question adequately, you might say,

"Well, I think that brings us to the next question."

If you need to linger on the first question, say nothing about the out-of-order response until after you've read the next question. Then, acknowledge that it has been answered (at least in part). If more discussion is warranted, you could ask,

"How about a different thought than the one Mary shared?"

If Mary's answer was complete, you can say,

"Well, I think Mary answered that for us, so there's no need to cover this again."

A person's answer is unscriptural or completely unrelated to the question.

> ▸ Thank the person without agreeing, then call on the most knowledgeable/reliable member in your group to answer.

"Thank you, John. Sam, how did you answer this?"

If the group has bonded and the person who answers wrongly isn't generally timid, you might, first, ask him or her for a Bible reference and/or to share which Bible translation they are using. Sometimes, confusion arises from different wording in different translations. Doing this takes the focus off the group member (who may feel embarrassed) and puts the focus back on the Scripture. If the same individual's answers are repeatedly drawn from their denominational or political ideologies, consider soliciting their help (privately, after the group time) in keeping the group focused on the Biblical text by sharing specific references or passages from among those given to support their answers, rather than citing outside sources.

The same individual begins to be the "first responder" to a question for the third time in a row.

> ▸ Say the person's name to halt them (with a smile). Then, follow immediately with, *"Let's first allow someone we haven't heard from yet (or recently)."* If this problem continues, in the following week's opening statement, give this quick reminder:

"Since we're aiming for a well-balanced discussion, if you've had one or two opportunities to share your answers, let's allow others the same opportunity before giving additional input."

Someone answers a question with research they've done through commentaries or with the thoughts of others (the teachings from their pastor or a book they've read).

> ▸ After the person has shared, thank them but then ask what personal insights they had. In the following week's opening statement, you might remind the group that you want to hear their own thoughts on the questions, not the ideas they've heard or read about. If one person does this continually, privately and genuinely applaud their interest and desire to grow their knowledge. Ask them to help you *"level the playing field"* in the group by leaving information out of their answers that they heard or read from someone else, since not everyone in the group has time or access to such information.

The discussion of a particular question is important, but no one is answering (or very few are answering).

- Most discussion leaders experience the temptation to allow the group to determine the amount of time spent discussing each question, giving more time when the group has much to say and less when they say little. However, it's unlikely that group members have thought, in advance, about the potential spiritual benefit of discussing each question, as you have when creating your time-guide. They may have a lot to say about interesting but less spiritually impactful questions, while saying little about a life-application question. In order for the group to benefit from your prayerful planning, you'll need to become comfortable with some silence and use techniques to prompt more discussion, if the question is an important one. In the case of a life-application question, try sharing your own answer as a way of spurring on other sharing. You can also say,

    "I really think this is worth talking about. I'd like to hear from at least four of you. Who will be first?"

A group member speaks in a way that is inappropriate.

- It is possible a group member might use disparaging labels, share gossip, make specific and intimate sexual references, criticize a minister, parachurch organization or denomination, or say something equally inappropriate. Some of these situations are uncommon, but if they occur, they can be very awkward for the entire group. Interrupt the person by speaking their name. Then, you might respond in one of these ways:

    "I'm concerned that you are sharing something we perhaps shouldn't hear, and so I think we better move on."

    "I'm concerned you're sharing something you might later wish you hadn't shared, and so I think we better move on."

    (In the case of church/ministerial criticism) "Since we come from a variety of backgrounds, we want to be sure we're respectful of everyone's perspectives, so let's move on."

    Occasionally, inappropriate sharing occurs simply because an individual lacks social skill e.g., dominating the group with long, dramatic stories about their circumstances or someone else's life, etc. You might ask your co-leader (assuming you have one) to take the person to another room and pray with them. Of course, this approach is dependent on advanced preparation for such a circumstance. If you do not have a co-leader, you might ask one of the more mature and trustworthy members of your group to be ready to take this role. However, *only do this if your co-leader is of the same gender as the person who needs personal attention.* You might say,

    "This sounds like something I would like [co-leader] to pray with you about right now in the [name a space you and your co-leader have prearranged for this purpose]."

    On a very rare occasion, an attendee may have needs that cannot be met by the group e.g., someone whose mental illness or lack of self-awareness is regularly disruptive. For the benefit of the group, you should not allow this to continue. Ask your pastor or another mature believer to pray with you, and then, speak to the troubled person about the goals of the group. As kindly as you can, tell them you do not think the group can meet their needs. Please do not attempt to have this conversation alone if you believe the individual may physically harm you. Seek the assistance of a pastor or experienced counselor.

    If the group member is emotional, you, as the leader, should take the time to pray aloud for the hurting person on the spot, before resuming the discussion. To get back on track, it's possible you may need to pass over one or two questions (use your best judgment), but doing so is preferable to shortening the group prayer time or skipping the video.

GROUP ATMOSPHERE

A group member asks a question about the passage that is not among those in the workbook/lesson.

> However interesting the subject and however prepared you may be to answer, the moment you allow a diversion you've set a precedent. After this, the group will assume they can introduce additional questions or subjects. Explain the need to stick to the given questions in order to get through the lesson on time, while affirming the individual's curiosity and reminding everyone that there is no limit to the number of good questions that can be discussed about any passage.
>
> *"What a good question! I imagine we could probably talk for hours about these passages. Christa (address questioner directly with good eye contact), let's wait and see if this gets addressed in the video. If not, maybe you and I can do some research this coming week. Okay, we're on question number..."*

A group member repeatedly asks you for the answers to the questions.

> Ideally, you explained that your role is to facilitate discussion and not to teach the first time your group met (see Opening Statement, p. 130). Nevertheless, it is not uncommon for group members to unintentionally test you in this. If one or more individuals continue to ask for your answers or clarification of an answer, reply with the discussion leaders' favorite fallback:
>
> *"Let's see if this is clarified for us in the video."*

You don't sense your class members are responding well to you, you don't feel qualified as a leader, and/or you are generally discouraged about leading.

> Praise the Lord for a humbling opportunity to grow. Confess any known sin to Him and immediately begin to obey in that area. Ask the Holy Spirit for wisdom (James 1:5) and re-read the Leaders' Guide to see if you might have missed something. Trust the Lord that your feelings are not always an accurate reflection of reality. PERSEVERE!

Your group attendance is down.

> It's always wise to contact people who are absent two consecutive weeks without explanation. Regardless of their reason, if they don't think they were missed they may be tempted not to return. In addition, develop a personal habit of praying for each person in your discussion group by name at least once during the week. You might also pray for the challenges of regular attendance in your group prayer time (acknowledge that the request is not for yourself, but explain that it is for the group as a whole). You might also name the people who are absent and ask the group to let them know they were missed if they see them during the week.

The group is quiet and lacks the intimacy for which you're aiming.

> First and foremost, ask the Lord to give you wisdom. Then, look around the room in which you meet. The degree to which the environment sets a tone can be surprising. As much as possible, arrange the seating so your group is in a tight, round circle. Ensure each chair is positioned so that the person who occupies it can easily see the face of everyone else in the group. Oblong or square sitting arrangements prohibit people who are sharing from being fully seen by those who sit alongside them. Solicit your group's help in pushing away or removing chairs that remain empty once you begin. These "dead spaces" are isolating. Avoid sitting around a table, as it, subconsciously, becomes a barrier, as well. It's also important to consider the tone of your voice and your body language. Speaking too softly or too loudly will not invite engagement. Do you smile often? Finally, speak privately and lovingly (but directly) to group members who have made more than one offensive remark, are domineering, or regularly want to offer the others advice. This can quickly shut down a group.

PERSONAL APPLICATION

Someone fails to grasp the significance of applying the life application questions to their present life, and instead, regularly refers to an impactful situation from their past.

- Life-application questions are ultimately the most important. Many in this study specifically ask for a recent or current application. Some Christians find it particularly tempting to dwell on the big ways (or one big way) in which God worked in their life in the past. When asked how God has helped them, shown Himself in their life, or something similar, the individual goes back to that one situation or time in their life, again and again. It may be that God intervened in a way that was particularly dramatic on that occasion, even miraculous, or that it was a time of intense trauma that marked their life (i.e., cancer, divorce, death of a family member, etc.).

  One of the many ways that Christian leaders can be helpful is by continually challenging those for whom they have responsibility to try and see how God is working in their life in the present - for, surely, He is!

  If you are having this issue in your group, you might try acknowledging (right after you read the question) that God's recent involvement may not be as dramatic as it was on an occasion in the distant past. Tell the group that you, nevertheless, hope the question made them aware of God's present involvement in their life. You might say this is true of yourself:

  "I find it has been really helpful for me to think about God's recent involvement in my life because it keeps me aware that His work in me is always ongoing."

  If someone in the group still fails to grasp the importance of this and their answers don't reflect a sense that God is presently at work in them, you may have to follow up their answer with,

  "Thank you. And did you also think of any way God has recently helped you?"

After answering personal application questions OR during the prayer time, one or more group members tend to give the others advice.

- The advice-giver may have very pure intentions. Nevertheless, most of us appreciate a "safe place" to share our struggles without necessarily being told how to handle them. Often, we already know what we ought to do and just want to honestly share about or request prayer over our struggle to do it. The best way to handle this is to suggest, in your first meeting or during one of your opening statements, that the group becomes a "safe place" to share. Then, clarify, asking them directly to avoid advice-giving unless, of course, someone asks for advice. The earlier in the study you do this the better. If a struggling person gets unwanted advice, they may shut down and refuse to share personal things in the future or worse yet--not return. If a group member asks for advice, you should be the first to respond, saying,

  "I wouldn't be surprised if someone has a good suggestion. Would a few of you reach out to (so-and-so) this week?"

TIME MANAGEMENT

The discussion of a particular question is exuberant and interesting, but much more time is being spent on it than you planned.

▶ If much more time is being spent on a question than you planned, you'll need to firmly but graciously interrupt and explain the need to move on.

> *"Wow, great discussion on question #7, everyone. I know we could say a lot more about this, but we may not get to the last question or someone's favorite if we don't move on. Question #8 says, ..."*

If it's one individual's answer that goes on for an extended time, you may need to politely interrupt them (speak their name to get their attention) and say something like,

> *"Susan, those are all great points, but would you mind if I stopped you there since I think some of what you're saying may be covered in a later question? Thanks for the great segue!"*

Then, try to find something later in the discussion to tie back to what they were saying and affirm them.

In the week leading up to your meeting, a group member has had a traumatizing experience e.g., lost his or her job, lost a loved one in death, divorce, or separation, etc. and shares about this (perhaps at length) in the course of the discussion.

▶ If the group member appears relatively calm, express sympathy (*"Wow, I'm so sorry to hear this."*). Then, ask his or her permission to include the situation in the usual group prayer time. (Make sure to follow through. Once it's time for group prayer, ask the individual exactly how they would like the group to pray.)

If the group member is emotional, take the time to pray aloud for the hurting person on the spot (you should be the one to pray), before resuming the discussion. To get back on track, it's possible you may need to pass over one or two questions (use your best judgment), but doing so is preferable to shortening the group prayer time or skipping the video.

PRAYER TIME

A person prays "in tongues" during prayer time.

- Interrupt immediately by saying, *"Is there someone able to interpret this?"* If not, ask the pray-er politely to discontinue, since 1 Corinthians 14 forbids public prayer in tongues without interpretation.

During the discussion, a group member suggests praying (either immediately or during the prayer time) over a personal matter that was shared by someone else, without requesting the sharer's permission.

- Give the individual who shared their personal situation a way to agree that they would like prayer OR to move on without group prayer, if they are not ready for that. With a compassionate smile and tone, thank the person who suggested prayer (so they are not embarrassed for making the suggestion), saying,

    "That is very thoughtful, [name]. We definitely want to pray for [Sharer's name], if he/she is willing. Let's see what, if anything, he/she requests when it's time to pray."

After answering personal application questions OR during the prayer time, one or more group members tend to give the others advice.

- The advice-giver may have very pure intentions. Nevertheless, most of us appreciate a "safe place" to share our struggles without necessarily being told how to handle them. Often, we already know what we ought to do and just want to honestly share about or request prayer over our struggle to do it. The best way to handle this is to suggest, in your first meeting or during one of your opening statements, that the group becomes a "safe place" to share. Then, clarify, asking them directly to avoid advice-giving unless, of course, someone asks for advice. The earlier in the study you do this the better. If a struggling person gets unwanted advice, they may shut down and refuse to share personal things in the future or worse yet--not return. If a group member asks for advice, you should be the first to respond, saying,

    "I wouldn't be surprised if someone has a good suggestion. Would a few of you reach out to (so-and-so) this week?"

Lesson 1 Answers

Day 1 - *Refer to Joshua 1:1-11.*

1 Read Genesis 12:1-7 and 15:13-21. What promises had God given Abraham, the Patriarch of the nation of Israel?

In Genesis 12, God promised Abraham numerous descendants, blessings, and land. In Genesis 15, God promised that, after 400 years of enslavement in a foreign land, He would deliver Abraham's descendants, punish their oppressors, and bring them out with many possessions. In the fourth generation, Abraham's descendants would return and possess the land of the Canaanites.

2 Read Joshua 1:1-6 with Genesis 46:2-4, Exodus 1:1-7, 12:40-41, and Numbers 32:13. From these passages and what you discovered in question 1, give a short history of the Israelites (Abraham's descendants) ending with the Joshua 1 passage.
Note: Abraham's grandson Jacob is also known as "Israel."

After God promised Abraham numerous descendants, blessings, and land, He directed Abraham's grandson Jacob, also known as Israel, to take his family to Egypt, where God promised to grow his family into a great nation. God also promised He would bring them back out of Egypt to Canaan. According to Exodus 1, Jacob's 12 sons went to Egypt and became exceedingly numerous. According to Exodus 12, after 430 years, the Israelites left Egypt. According to Numbers 32, the generation of Israelites that left Egypt spent 40 years wandering in the desert until they died. Joshua 1 says that following the death of Moses, God appointed Joshua to lead the children of those Israelites who died in the desert in overtaking and possessing Canaan, the Promised Land.

3 What challenges and promises did God give Joshua (Joshua 1:1-11), and how can you apply one or more of them to your own circumstances today?

Challenges: "Get ready to cross the Jordan River into the land I am about to give to them" (1:2); "Be strong and very courageous...do not be terrified or discouraged" (1:6, 7, 9); "Be careful to obey the law so you may be successful... meditate on it day and night" (1:7, 8). Promises: "I will give you every place where you set your foot" (1:3); "No one will be able to stand up against you all the days of your life" (1:5); "As I was with Moses, so I will be with you; I will never leave you nor forsake you... The Lord your God will be with you wherever you go" (1:5, 9). [Personal sharing regarding challenges and promises]

Day 2 - *Refer to Joshua 1:12-2:24.*

4 Read Joshua 1:2, 12-18 with Numbers 32:1-2, 5, 16-22 and record the basic facts about the land inheritance of the tribes of Reuben, Gad, and the half tribe of Manasseh. How does Joshua 1 say these tribes responded to his reminder of their obligation?

Two-and-a-half of the 12 tribes had asked Moses to allow them to inherit the land east of the Jordan, formerly belonging to the Amorite kings, Sihon and Og. They believed the land was spacious enough for their vast flocks and herds. Moses' agreement was contingent upon their willingness to assist the other nine-and-a-half tribes in conquering Canaan, west of the Jordan. According to the agreement, they could not return to their land inheritance until all of the tribes received their inheritance. While those men of fighting age were engaged, the families and flocks of the two-and-a-half tribes could remain east of the Jordan. In Joshua 1:12-18, the eastern tribes affirmed their intentions to keep the promise they had made to Moses and fully submit to Joshua's leadership.

5 How did Rahab explain her reason for helping the two Israelite spies? What do Rahab's words and actions cause you to conclude about her faith? Include verse numbers with your answers.

In 2:9-11, Rahab said, "I know that the LORD has given this land to you and that a great fear of you has fallen on us, so that all who live in this country are melting in fear because of you. We have heard how the LORD dried up the water of the Red Sea for you when you came out of Egypt, and what you did to Sihon and Og, the two kings of the Amorites east of the Jordan, whom you completely destroyed. When we heard of it, our hearts melted and everyone's courage failed because of you, for the LORD your God is God in heaven above and on the earth below." Rahab had come to believe that the God of the Israelites was the same God who made heaven and earth. She chose to assist the Israelites, believing their God intended to overthrow her own city-state and give it to them. She hoped that the Israelites would accept her as one of their own and spare her life and the lives of her family members. By aligning herself with the Israelites, Rahab chose to honor the Israelites and the God of the Israelites over her own people and their gods.

6 According to Joshua 2:1, what was Rahab's occupation? With this in mind, glance at Matthew 1:1, 5 and explain how Rahab has been honored. What does this tell you about the God of the Bible? See 1 Corinthians 1:26-31.

Rahab was a woman in a patriarchal society, a Gentile despised by Jews, and a prostitute, yet she was privileged to be in the ancestral line of Jesus Christ! The God of the Bible does not show favoritism. He used the descendants of Abraham as His instruments of blessing to the world because through them, Jesus Christ descended and the Holy Scriptures have been handed down, but God has always intended to include the Gentiles in His plan of salvation (Galatians 3:8). 1 Corinthians 1:26-31 says that God intentionally chooses to work through unlikely people in order that He might be glorified.

7 Whom will you commit to pray for this week that, like Rahab, they might shift their allegiance to the Lord, God of heaven and earth?

[Personal sharing]

Day 3 - *Refer to Joshua 3 and 4*

8 Skim Exodus 25:1-22, Numbers 10:33-36, and Deuteronomy 10:8. Record what you learn about the Ark of the Covenant.

The Israelites donated specific items that Moses used to build a portable sanctuary, God's dwelling, according to the pattern shown him on the mountain. One of the Tabernacle's furnishings, the Ark of the Covenant, was a chest, overlaid with gold and with rings built into both ends, enabling it to be carried on poles. The lid or "atonement cover" had two cherubim facing one another and mounted atop. The Ark of the Covenant contained the "Testimony," which was the stone tablets with the covenant law written on them, Aaron's budding rod (Numbers 17:1-11), and a manna-filled urn (Exodus 16:33-34). Symbolically, God dwelt between the wings of the two cherubim, and there Moses met with Him. Throughout the 40-year journey from Sinai to the Promised Land, The Levites, who were the priestly tribe, carried the Ark. Wherever the Israelites went, the Ark went before them, leading the way (Numbers 10:33-36).

9 Based on what you learned in question 8, why would Joshua have sent out instructions to follow the Ark in Joshua 3:2-4? Why would he have wanted the Israelites to also keep their distance? For students who are familiar with New Testament teachings, explain how a person today can "draw near" to God's presence. Refer to Hebrews 10:19-22.

Wherever the Israelites went during their 40 years of wilderness wandering, the Ark, the place of God's symbolic dwelling, always led the way. The Israelites were told to follow the Ark because following it meant following God (Joshua 3). He would lead them safely into places that were unfamiliar to them (verse 4). However, in reverence to the Lord their King, they were also to keep their distance. Their sin was a barrier that kept them from safely approaching God's holy presence. As a reminder, the Law of Moses (also Joshua 3:4) instructed Old Testament believers to keep a physical distance between their bodies and the things of God. Nevertheless, in every era, people have experienced intimacy with God by faith. Jesus' shed blood paved the way for open access to God's presence (Hebrews 10:19). Previously, access to God was indirect, through the intervention of sacrifices and a priest. Those whose sins have been forgiven are legally justified before God through faith in Jesus and can directly approach ("draw near to") Him.

10 See Joshua 3:4. Is there some "territory" that you can trust God to lead you through at this time in your life, since "you have never been this way before"? If so, what is it?

[Personal sharing]

Day 4 - *Refer to Joshua 3 and 4.*

11 List all the reasons why God miraculously stopped the flow of the Jordan River during its flood stage to allow the Israelites to cross on dry land.

The miracle was a physical provision to make possible the crossing of a river in flood stage by an entire nation of people. Indeed, this was a generation that had grown up in the desert, a good distance from any place where they could have learned to swim! Additionally, the Lord performed this miracle to give the Israelites confidence in Joshua, their newly appointed leader (3:7; 4:14), to know the living God was among them and would drive out the inhabitants of Canaan (3:10), to remind their descendants of His power in bringing them into the Land of Promise (4:6-7, 21-23), "that the people of the earth [my emphasis] might know that the hand of the Lord is powerful," and "that you might always fear the Lord your God" (4:23-24).

12 Refer to Joshua 4:6 and 21. What has God done in your life recently that you ought to share with someone, so that they might delight in His awesome deeds? It does not need to be as dramatic as the crossing of the Jordan on dry ground!

[Personal sharing]

Day 5 - *Refer to Joshua 5:1-12.*

13 What two events occurred at Gilgal after the Israelites had crossed into the Promised Land but before they began to conquer it?

All the Israelite men of this younger generation were circumcised and the Passover was celebrated.

14 From Joshua 1:1-5:12, list all the events that should have prepared the Israelites for the conquest of the Promised Land. Explain your reasoning.

In chapter 1, the agreement of the eastern tribes to keep their commitment to cross the Jordan, fight with the others, and obey Joshua enabled the Israelites to be united in their effort. It also brought encouragement to the other ten-and-a-half tribes. The Israelites would have also been encouraged to know the Canaanites were already demoralized and terrorized by God's acts on Israel's behalf, information the spies received from Rahab in chapter 2. In chapter 3, the miraculous crossing of the Jordan River was a reminder of God's power and assured Israel of His intention of giving them the land. If God could get an entire nation of people across a major river at its flood stage on dry ground, couldn't He also give them the land? In 4:14, the exaltation of Joshua as God's chosen leader left the Israelites in awe of Joshua and gave them great confidence in his leadership. In chapter 5, the observances of circumcision, a symbol of cutting off one's own strength and relying on God, and the Passover, at God's command, prepared Israel spiritually for conquest, because obedience precedes success (Joshua 1:8). The Passover was also a specific reminder of God's mighty acts on their behalf in their past.

15 Reread Joshua 1:8. How does reading, meditating on, and obeying God's word prepare you for spiritual victory? Can you think of a way that it can help you gain victory this week?

Joshua 1:8 commends study and meditation on God's word as essential to spiritual victory (prosperity and success). A person must be familiar with God's word in order to fully obey it. We must always have it in the forefronts of our minds, because obedience is foreign to our sin nature. The truth in God's word renews our minds so we can discover God's will for us (Romans 12:2). [Personal sharing]

Lesson 2 Answers

Day 1 - *Refer to Joshua 5:13-Joshua 6*

1. Give your opinion about the identity of the mysterious "Commander of the Army of the Lord" in Joshua 5:13-15. For help, compare Genesis 18:2 with Genesis 18:22 and 19:1. Also compare Genesis 32:24 with Genesis 32:30, and see Numbers 22:23, 31, 1 Chronicles 21:16, and Revelation 19:11-16.

The Old Testament contains a number of instances where the Lord seemed to manifest Himself in some physical form. Bible scholars refer to such divine self-revelations as theophanies or "Christophanies," based on the reasoning that the second person of the Trinity, Jesus Christ, is the only person of the Godhead known to have put on flesh. Just as a "man" appeared to Joshua, a "man" also appeared to Abraham and to Jacob, and in the latter instances, the text identifies the "man" as the Lord. Some Bible students believe that Joshua met an angelic messenger, but the "Commander of the Lord's Army" was more likely the same One sometimes called the "Angel of the Lord" (a Christophany). The facts that the "man" whom Joshua met received Joshua's worship (Joshua 5:14) and said that Joshua was standing on holy ground (Joshua 5:15) are consistent with the opinion that the "Commander of the Lord's Army" was the Lord Jesus Himself. According to Revelation 19, at the end of this age, Jesus will lead the armies of heaven in battle with a drawn sword.

2. From Joshua 6, describe the Israelites' strategy in overthrowing Jericho. Was this a military strategy a human commander would be likely to devise?

The Israelites marched around the city of Jericho once a day for six days. An armed guard led the way, followed by seven priests sounding seven trumpets, the Ark of the Lord, and a rear guard. Except for the sound of the trumpets, they marched in eerie silence and returned to their camp for the night. On the seventh day, the procession marched around the city seven times. At the sounding of a long trumpet blast and Joshua's signal, the Israelites gave a loud shout and the walls around the city collapsed. They charged in, destroyed every living thing with the sword, except for Rahab and her household, and burned the city. Any object that would not burn, such as those made from precious metals, was put in the treasury of the Lord. From a human perspective, the strategy was insane, but ultimately, it proved that the judgment was God's judgment, carried out by His power and under His authority.

3. Read Ephesians 6:12-18. What battle are you fighting that may involve spiritual warfare?

[Personal sharing]

Day 2 - *Refer to Joshua 6.*

4. Imagine being a resident of Jericho and observing the processional around the city day after day for seven days! What would have gone through your mind? See Joshua 2:8-13, 5:1.

On each of the seven days Israel marched around Jericho, its inhabitants were given yet another opportunity to repent. Surely they were terrified by the prospect of imminent death, yet apparently, no one repented. Each resident could have followed Rahab's example and thrown him or herself at the mercy of Israel's God, but they did not. Joshua 11:20 indicates that once the Canaanites repeatedly refused to repent of their own will, God passed judgment by hardening their hearts, revoking any further opportunity.

5. According to Romans 1:18-20 and 2:14-16, by what means do all people possess certain knowledge about God? What further knowledge about God did the Canaanite/Amorite peoples possess? See Joshua 2:10 and 5:1.

All people possess some general knowledge of God through nature (creation) and through their consciences. The Canaanites also knew of God's miracles in bringing Israel out of Egypt, His deliverance at the Red Sea, the more recent victories He had given them against Sihon and Og, and how He enabled them to cross the Jordan River on dry ground during its flood stage.

6. From Leviticus 11:44-45, what is God's righteous standard? What is the deserved consequence of our sin according to Genesis 2:17-19, Romans 1:32, 5:12, 6:23, 8:13, Galatians 6:7-8, and James 1:15?

God's righteous standard is holiness and the deserved consequence of sin is death.

7. Revisit the following references from Lesson One and estimate the minimum number of years God patiently endured the Amorites' extreme depravity (sin): Genesis 15:13-16, Exodus 12:40-41, and Numbers 32:13.

A minimum of 600 years: Roughly 200 years in which the Patriarchs lived in Canaan, 430 years in which the Israelites lived in Egypt, and another 40 years in which the Israelites wandered in the wilderness.

8. It is difficult for us to think about the destruction of an entire city.

(a) Can you think of a reason why it was necessary, and perhaps even merciful, for God to order the deaths of the young along with the old? See Romans 2:6, Hebrews 4:13, 9:27, and Revelation 20:13.

It is difficult to accept the slaying of young children along with responsible adults. God is not accountable to us for His judgments, but we know He is just. Over at least five generations, the Canaanites had proven that they were not moving toward God but away from Him. Any children spared would likely have carried their parents' pagan influence into yet another generation, and among other things, have been a snare to the Israelites. Considering the Bible's teaching about future judgment, perhaps God was merciful in bringing swift death on the Canaanite children. Those who live short lives will have less for which to be accountable than those who have lived long but immoral lives. Our eternal condition is far more important than length of life on earth.

(b) According to Romans 3:10-11, 23 and 1 Peter 3:18, who has ever deserved God's mercy and what provision has God made for our salvation?

No one has ever deserved God's mercy. All have sinned. God has mercifully provided a means of salvation by Christ's substitutionary death for our sins.

(c) Read Titus 3:5. If you have experienced God's mercy and salvation through personal faith in Jesus Christ, how will you express your thanks to Him today? If you have not, what exactly is holding you back from receiving Jesus as your Savior and Lord this very moment? What assurance do you have that your life will not end and you will stand before God this very day?

[Personal sharing]

Day 3 - *Refer to Joshua 6-8.*

9 Skim Joshua 7 and 8. See especially 7:1-12, 20-21, 24-26 and 8:1-2, 20-22.

    a) Explain the events that resulted in Israel's humiliating defeat at Ai.

    In direct disobedience to God's orders, an Israelite named Achan coveted, took, and hid some of the "devoted things" at Jericho. His direct disobedience was the cause of Israel's defeat at Ai. God is serious about sin, holiness, and absolute obedience to His commands.

    b) Revisit Joshua 7:12. In what way does this verse explain the problem? What specifically did God say He required of Israel in order that He would be with them and grant them victory against Ai?

    The Israelites were God's chosen instruments of justice. Their war was a holy war. However, because of Achan's sin, the Israelites themselves were "liable to destruction." In order for the Lord to be with them in battle, they had to purge their camp of sin by destroying all that was "devoted to destruction."

10 Read Joshua 8:30-35 with Deuteronomy 27:1-13 and 28:1-2, 15. After Israel occupied key cities in central Canaan, they renewed their covenant with the Lord as Moses had instructed. According to the verses in Deuteronomy 28, why was it important for Joshua to recite the book of the Law in the presence of all Israel?

The Israelites needed to be reminded of what God required, since obedience to the His commands would result in His blessing and disobedience in cursing.

11 Read 1 John 1:8-2:6. In light of the passage, what attitudes toward sin and obedience should characterize believers? Do you currently need to adjust any of your attitudes?

The passage teaches that no one is without sin, but when we confess our sin to God, He forgives and purifies us through Jesus. Rather than persisting in sinful patterns, those who belong to God should be characterized by an obedience that is motivated by gratitude and love. We should be humble since we are sinners, grateful for God's provision in Jesus, and eager to please and obey Him. [Personal sharing]

Day 4 - *Refer to Joshua 9.*

12 Read Joshua 9:1-6, 14-27. What does verse 24 reveal about the degree to which the Gibeonites understood who ordered their destruction?

The Gibeonites "were clearly told" that the Lord Himself had commanded Moses to wipe out all the inhabitants of the land.

13 What explanation for Israel's failure with regard to the Gibeonites is given in Joshua 9:14? Is there a matter you have recently considered too unimportant or unnecessary to pray about and assumed your own good judgment would suffice?

The men of Israel did not inquire of the Lord to find out if they should make a treaty with the Gibeonites or not. [Personal sharing]

Day 5 - *Refer to Joshua 10-12.*

14 Read Joshua 10:1-15, 42 and 11:1-8, 15. Using these verses, summarize Joshua's campaigns in southern and northern Canaan.

Joshua defeated the Amorite kings who made war against him in the south and in the north. In both cases, after Joshua heard from the Lord, he initiated a "sudden" or "surprise" attack. The five kings of the south--the king of Jerusalem appears to have been their leader (Joshua 10:1, 3)—were incensed by Gibeon's treaty with Joshua. When they attacked Gibeon, Joshua attacked them. It was in this campaign that the "sun stood still in the sky" (Joshua 10:12-13). Then, at the king of Hazor's initiative (11:1, 10), the northern kings led an army "as numerous as the sand on the seashore" against Joshua (Joshua 11:5), but again, the Lord gave Joshua victory.

15 Reread Joshua 10:9-14.

a How do these verses illustrate the interplay between human effort and divine involvement?

This passage portrays the Israelites' effort and the Lord's mighty arm accomplishing the victory. The Israelites marched all night to engage the five southern kings (10:9), 25 miles up a 4,000 foot ascent, but the Lord threw their enemies into confusion and gave Israel victory (10:10). While Israel pursued the enemy, God hurled down large hailstones (10:10-11). Joshua asked the Lord to make the sun stand still (10:12), and the Lord listened and did it (10:14). He was fighting for Israel.

b What effort is currently being demanded of you that you will trust God to divinely oversee?

[Personal sharing]

Lesson 3 Answers

Day 1 - *Refer to Joshua 13.*

1 Israel had completed major military campaigns victoriously in the Promised Land. According to Joshua 13:1 and 13:6b-7, what two objectives still lay before them?

13:1 says there were still "very large areas of land to be taken over" and 13:6b-7 indicates that the land still had to be allocated among the tribes.

2 Among the description of the land deeded to the tribes of Reuben, Gad, and the half-tribe of East Manasseh, Joshua twice stated that another tribe, Levi, did not receive a land inheritance within Canaan's borders. According to Joshua 13:14, 13:33, 18:7 and Numbers 18, why didn't they?

According to Numbers 18, the Levites did not need to work land for their main source of food and income. Their God-assigned work was in the Tabernacle, which later became the Temple, and for this work they were compensated with the offerings the Israelites brought as sacrifices. This included anything "devoted" to the Lord: all the oil, wine, and grain offered as "firstfruits" to the Lord as well as the Israelites' tithes. Joshua 13:14 also says that the food offerings made to the Lord "by fire" were the Levites' inheritance. Joshua 13:33 indicates that the Lord Himself was their inheritance.

3 What personal obstacle did Joshua face (13:1) and what assurance did he receive that this problem was not a problem for God (13:6)? What seemingly impossible task will you ask God to handle for you?

13:1 says Joshua was well advanced in years, but in 13:6, God assured him that He Himself would drive out the remaining inhabitants of the land. [Personal sharing]

Day 2 - *Refer to Joshua 14-19.*

4 Joshua 14-19 records the tracts of land deeded to the remaining nine-and-a-half tribes west of the Jordan in Canaan. Based on any knowledge you have about the first five books of the Bible, why were the recording of these deeds and the receiving of the land causes for great rejoicing in Israel?

Hundreds of years earlier, God had promised the Patriarchs that their descendants would possess the land of Canaan as a permanent inheritance. Although that did not occur in the Patriarchs' lifetimes, they believed God would be faithful to His promise and were even buried in Canaan as a statement of their faith. Since their time, many generations of Israelites over a 430-year period had spent their lives enslaved in Egypt. Yet another generation had wandered in the desert. All of these people had anticipated the fulfillment of God's promise. After all these years, for each family to finally receive an allotted inheritance was cause for great rejoicing!

5 Read Numbers 14:6-25, and then skim Numbers 13 and 14:26-38 for information about Caleb. According to Numbers 14:30 and Joshua 14:10-11, what promise did God make and fulfill, and how did He bless Caleb even beyond what He had promised?

Caleb and Joshua were two of the 12 spies sent into Canaan by Moses to explore the land 45 years earlier (Joshua 14:10). 10 of the 12 spies doubted God could overthrow the intimidating inhabitants of the land. The Israelites believed this bad report and refused to enter Canaan. God punished them, causing all that generation to wander and die in the desert over a 40-year period. However, because Joshua and Caleb had trusted God, He promised that they alone would live to enter the Promised Land. At 85 years old, Caleb said that God had not only kept His promise to bring him into the land of Canaan, but He had also given him such good health that he was still as strong as he had been 45 years earlier! See Joshua 14:10-11.

6 Compare Caleb's courageous expansion of his territory (Joshua 15:13-19) to Ephraim and Manasseh's complaint that they were unable to take all their land (Joshua 17:14-18). Then, summarize Joshua's advice in Joshua 17:18b. Which person who depends on you for advice, guidance, or leadership could you similarly encourage?

While Caleb bravely expanded his territory beyond Hebron to Debir and the Negev, Ephraim and Manasseh complained that they did not have enough land because what they were given was being held by Canaanites with iron chariots. Joshua told them they needed to do the work of clearing the forested land they were given and of driving the Canaanites out from the plains. They could do it, he said. When difficult challenges come our way, it is always encouraging to have someone we respect say, "You can do it!" [Personal sharing]

7 Keeping in mind what you learned about the attitude of the tribes of Joseph (Ephraim and Manasseh) in question 6, read Joshua 15:63, 16:10, and 17:12-13.

a) What danger was war-weary Israel succumbing to and with what likely result? See Joshua 23:12-13.

It seems that the war-weary Israelites became lazy in their attitude toward driving out the Canaanites and reasoned that they could, instead, use them for slave labor. They started well but did not complete their God-given assignment. At the end of his life, Joshua warned them, just as Moses had, that the remaining Canaanites would eventually ensnare them (Joshua 23).

b) Is there a stronghold of sin that you have dismissed as too difficult to dislodge from your life or not worth the effort? What does Philippians 1:6 say to encourage you?

[Personal sharing]

Day 3 - *Refer to Joshua 20-22.*

8 According to Joshua 20, what was the purpose of having "cities of refuge"? See also Numbers 35:9-16, 19.

The Israelites were to select and designate six Cities of Refuge, three on each side of the Jordan, "so that anyone who kills a person accidentally and unintentionally may flee there and find protection from the avenger of blood." People accused of murder could live safely in these cities while awaiting trial.

9 The allocation of 48 towns for the Levites (Joshua 21) completes the division of the land among the tribes. Read the summary in Joshua 21:43-45, along with Joshua 23:14, and explain what you learn about the Lord God from these verses. What specific issue does this encourage you in?

God is faithful to do all He promises. [Personal sharing]

10 Read the drama in Joshua 22. What fundamental concern was so great that it almost caused a civil war between the eastern and western tribes?

After commending the eastern tribes for keeping their commitment to settle the western tribes in their land and exhorting them to keep the Law of Moses, which was to love God, walk in His ways, obey His commands, hold fast to Him, and serve Him wholeheartedly, Joshua freed them to return to their land and families east of the Jordan. Shortly after their return, the western tribes discovered that they had built an imposing altar on the border between them, the Jordan. The eastern tribes had built it as a reminder of their right to worship at the Lord's altar, which was west of the Jordan, but the western tribes assumed it was built as a second altar for sacrifices, which the Law of Moses forbade. The western tribes rallied for civil war and confronted the eastern tribes with their "sin," reminding them that it would bring cursing on all of Israel. The eastern tribes assured them that they fully intended to remain loyal to the Lord and explained their reasoning: They had built the altar as a sign to future generations that, despite the geographical division created by the Jordan, they were fully part of the inheritance of the Lord and had the right to worship at the true and only legal altar in the west. This news brought great relief and rejoicing among the western tribes. They praised God and ended any discussion of civil war. Their fundamental concern had been that if the eastern tribes had broken the Law of Moses, all the tribes would have suffered.

Day 4 - *Refer to Joshua 23-24.*

11 List the instructions and warnings Joshua gave Israel at the end of his life (chapter 23).

Joshua told Israel to expect God to drive out the remaining inhabitants and take possession of the land (23:5), to be very strong and careful to obey the law completely (23:6), to not associate with the nations that remain or to flirt with or serve their gods (23:7), to hold fast to the Lord (23:8), and to be careful to love the Lord (23:11). He warned that if they turned from God and allied with the remaining inhabitants, God would no longer drive them out but would allow them to be snares until they perished from the good land (23:12-13). He also warned that if they served other gods, God's threatened curses would surely fall on them (23:15-16).

12 According to Joshua 24, Joshua summoned the Israelites to renew their covenant agreement with God. What was the significance of choosing Shechem as the site for the ceremony? See Genesis 12:6-7. According to Joshua 24:32, what other significant event took place at Shechem, presumably during Joshua's lifetime?

Genesis 12:6 says that Abraham was in Shechem when he first received the promise that he would inherit Canaan. Shechem was also the site where Joseph's bones were buried. In accordance with Joseph's deathbed request, the Israelites had taken his bones with them when they left Egypt.

13 According to Joshua 24, what choice did Israel face? Include verse numbers. Specifically, how does this same choice challenge your life today?

According to Joshua 24:15, Joshua challenged the Israelites to make a serious decision about whether or not they would follow the Lord God. The alternative was to follow the false gods of their forefathers, like those Abraham's father Terah had worshipped "beyond the river" (Euphrates) or the gods of the local residents, the Amorites, in whose land they were living. [Personal sharing]

Day 5 - *Refer to Joshua 24.*

14 Which phrase in Joshua 24:31 explains Israel's faithfulness during the years Joshua's contemporaries remained alive?

They "had experienced [known] everything the Lord had done for Israel." They had personally witnessed God miraculously holding back the waters of the Jordan and they had witnessed Him fighting on their behalf.

15 What have you personally witnessed the Lord do for you that you need to share with your spiritual and physical descendants?

[Personal sharing]

Lesson 4 Answers

Day 1 - *Refer to Judges 1-2.*

1 Read what Judges 1:1-3 and Joshua 19:1 say about the tribes of Judah and Simeon. Then, look back at Jacob's prophetic blessings over his twelve sons on his deathbed (Genesis 49). Explain how Judges 1:2-3 reveals a partial fulfillment of the prophecies about Judah and Simeon (Genesis 49:5-12).

Judges 1:2 reveals the tribe of Judah as God's chosen leader in the absence of an individual leader after Joshua's death. Jacob's prophecy (Genesis 49) portrays Judah as a leader over his brothers. Because of Simeon's geographical location within the boundaries of the land of Judah and the resulting relationship between the two tribes, eventually, Simeon was absorbed into Judah and lost its identity as a distinct tribe. In this sense, Simeon was "scattered," as foretold (Genesis 49:7).

2 Following the national campaigns that Joshua fought and won, Judges 1 reveals information about regional tribal battles that were fought to drive remaining inhabitants out of the Promised Land. How thoroughly did Israel cleanse the land of these people groups? See Judges 1:19, 21, 27-36 and 2:2-5.

The tribes of Judah, Benjamin, Manasseh, Ephraim, Zebulun, Asher, Naphtali, and Dan (seven-and-a-half tribes) are named among those who did not completely drive the Canaanite/Amorite inhabitants out of the land. Only nine-and-a-half tribes possessed land west of the Jordan and Simeon, one of the two not listed, by implication from verses 1-3, was included with the tribe of Judah. The Lord had confronted the Israelites, apparently prior to Joshua's death (2:2-7), about failing to break down the altars of these other people groups and entering into covenants with them. He had said He would no longer assist them in driving the former residents out of the land but would allow them to remain and become thorns and snares to Israel.

3 Judges 2:10-19 describes a cycle of apostasy (abandoning faith in God) that characterized Israel during the period of the Judges.

(a) Use the verses listed to fill in the missing words:

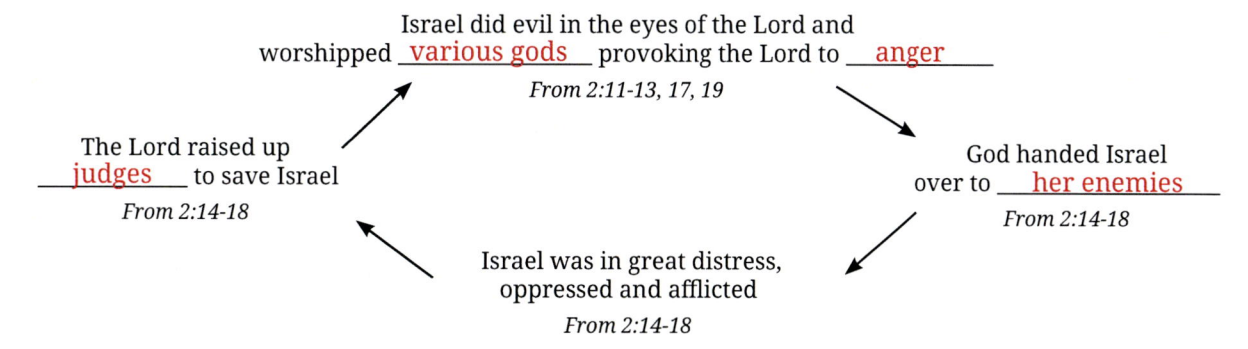

Israel did evil in the eyes of the Lord and worshipped __various gods__ provoking the Lord to __anger__
From 2:11-13, 17, 19

God handed Israel over to __her enemies__
From 2:14-18

Israel was in great distress, oppressed and afflicted
From 2:14-18

The Lord raised up __judges__ to save Israel
From 2:14-18

(b) What does 2:10-19 reveal about God's anger toward the Israelites?

God was angered by Israel's apostasy and idolatry (2:12-13). The Lord's anger caused Him to withdraw His hand of protection and divine enablement (2:14). The Lord's anger moved Him to thwart Israel's progress; He fought against them (2:15).

(c) What does 2:10-19 reveal about God's mercy toward the Israelites?

The Lord was willing to deliver His people when they were in distress (2:16) because He had compassion on them (2:18).

3

d. Which behaviors of the Israelites, as described in 2:10-19, are typical of people in every era who neither "know the Lord nor what He has done" (2:10)?

They do evil (2:11), substitute lesser gods for the true, living God (2:11-12), tend to follow what others around them are doing (2:12), are quick to abandon positive influences or instruction (2:17), and "refuse to give up their evil practices and stubborn ways" (2:19).

e. How will you use what you learn from this cycle to intercede in prayer for yourself or others?

This information certainly leaves us humbled and keenly aware of our need for God's mercy. It also gives some insight into the complexity of the relationship between human free will and God's sovereign control and election. We cannot help ourselves out of the bondage of human depravity--"refusal to give up their evil practices and stubborn ways"--yet responsibility for bondage and the sin that results is fully ours (2:12b-15). God is behind the scenes working alternately for and against us. He is angry about rebellion yet shows compassion and mercy. Such knowledge ought to move us to humbly ask God to work both for and against those who are in rebellion against Him so that they seek Him. The passage also evokes gratitude to the Lord for His gracious dealings with us and for rescuing us, since we cannot rescue ourselves. [Personal sharing]

Day 2 - *Refer to Judges 2-3.*

4. What reasons did God give for allowing the other nations to be left in the land after Joshua's death? See Judges 2:20-3:6.

To punish them for their apostasy (2:20-21), to test Israel's faithfulness (2:22, 3:4), and to give Israel experience in warfare (3:2).

5. See any text note in your Bible that clarifies the word translated "judge," for example, in Judges 2:16. What insight about the nature of this office is given in Judges 2:16, 18 and 3:9-10, 15-16, 31?

The judges were primarily military leaders (deliverers). However, Judges 4:5 indicates the judge Deborah held court. Samuel, the last Judge of Israel, was also a prophet (1 Samuel 3:20) and went on an annual circuit through Israel, "judging in all those places" (1 Samuel 7:16). Apparently, his leadership was spiritual, civil, and judicial.

6. Israel had many enemies.

a. Which three enemies of the Israelites are named in Judges 3:7-31 and who were the first three judges the Lord raised up to deliver Israel from them? Include verse numbers.

Aram (northwestern Mesopotamia) was Israel's enemy (3:8) and Caleb's nephew Othniel was Israel's first judge (3:9). Moab was Israel's enemy and Ehud the left-handed Benjamite was Israel's second judge (3:12). Philistia was Israel's enemy and Shagmar was Israel's third judge (3:31).

b. From Judges 4:2, 6:1-3, and 10:7, list the names of Israel's other enemies in this period.

Israel's other enemies in the time of the judges were Canaan (4:2), Midian (6:1), the Amalekites and other eastern peoples (6:3), and Amon (10:7).

c. What kind of personal, social, or spiritual enemies do you need to ask the Lord to deliver you from today? See John 15:18, Romans 8:8, and 1 Peter 5:8.

The believer's greatest enemies are the world, the sin nature, and the devil. [Personal sharing]

Day 3 - *Refer to Judges 4-5.*

7 Skim Judges 4-5. Why did Barak fail to receive the honor for defeating Sisera?

Barak said he would only obey the Lord's command to lead Israel to war against the Canaanites if Deborah went with him (4:8). Deborah told Barak, "Because of the way you are going about this, the honor will not be yours, for the Lord will hand Sisera over to a woman" (4:9). That woman was Jael (4:21). Barak put his confidence in Deborah instead of in the Lord.

8 How does the picture Deborah paints at the conclusion of her hymn of victory (Judges 5:31) give insight into the key to spiritual success, which eluded Israel in the days of the judges? See also Deuteronomy 6:5, Joshua 22:5, and Psalm 18:1, 119:132.

Deborah said, "May those who love you be like the sun when it rises in its strength" (5:31 [some translations use the term "friend" rather than "those who love you"]). The social, political, and spiritual strength that the Israelites lacked during the 400-year period of the judges could only be found in love for (friendship with) God. Deborah, a prophetess (4:4), knew that Israel needed a new heart, one that truly loved the Lord.

9 Read Jeremiah 31:31-33 and Hebrews 8:7-13, focusing on the word "heart." In consideration of these verses and what Deborah indicated at the end of her hymn, how should we pray about persistent patterns of sin in our own lives? Write out your prayer.

We are wise and scriptural when we ask God to change our hearts, to cause us to love Him more, and as a result, to find Him as our source of strength to overcome cycles of sin. We should pray, "God, cause me to love you far more than I love anything else." [Personal sharing]

Day 4 - *Refer to Judges 6-8.*

10 According to Judges 6:14-15, what was Gideon's main objection to leading the Israelites in battle against the oppressive Midianites? What do 1 Corinthians 1:27-29 and 2 Corinthians 12:9-10 have to say about this?

Gideon was riddled with fear. He saw himself and his family as weak. Corinthians says God chooses weak people intentionally so they will not boast in themselves but in God. Paul said he boasted in his weakness, for when he was weak in his own estimation, he was strong in the Lord.

11 What first step toward courage did the Lord ask Gideon to take in Judges 6:25-30?

The Lord had Gideon start close to home. He had him tear down his father's idol and altar and replace them with an altar to the Lord.

12 Judges 6:36-40 tells of Gideon requesting a miracle regarding a fleece he laid out overnight.

a Describe the scenario in Judges 6:36-40 when Gideon puts out the fleece.

Gideon asked the Lord for a very specific sign involving a fleece as proof the Lord would give him victory. If there was dew only on the fleece and the ground was dry, he would know God would use him to save Israel. After God answered him favorably, Gideon reversed the strategy, asking God to make the fleece dry and the ground wet. Again, God answered his request.

b Was Gideon testing God because he did not know God's will? If not, why might Gideon have tested God as he did?

Gideon knew God's will and had God's promise of assistance before he put out the fleece. He was not putting out a fleece to discover God's will. Since Gideon was so riddled with fear, it is possible he may have been looking for a way out of leading Israel in battle. He may have hoped to change God's will with his test. However, since Gideon very likely had semi-pagan notions about God, he may have simply lacked the confidence that God was able to do what He promised and been looking for a demonstration of God's power. If nothing else, Gideon was certainly weak and struggling and just needed confirmation.

12 (c) Consider whether Gideon's actions in creating this test are an example Christians should follow and record your thoughts.

Gideon's request for the miraculous is not a model for us to follow. God is not obligated to accommodate such requests, although apparently in this case, He was graciously willing. It is far better for us to ask God to give us the assurance we need without demanding the miraculous or anything too specific. Deuteronomy 6:16 tells us not to put the Lord to the test when we are unbelieving. We should never demand that God prove Himself. However, in taking his struggles to God in prayer, Gideon is a good model. When weak, we too should go to God in prayer.

13 According to Judges 7, what lesson did the Lord teach fearful Gideon and Israel about human weakness? What do you need to ask God for assurance and victory over?

The Lord told Gideon He did not want Israel to boast that she had saved herself from the Midianites in her own strength. Through a process of whittling down Israel's soldiers until only 300 remained, God showed the Israelites that He was their deliverer. Human strength is not needed for victory. Having God fight our battles is the key to victory. [Personal sharing]

Day 5 - *Refer to Judges 8-9.*

14 Read Judges 8:22-23, 29-31 with 9:1-6, 22-24, 42-57. What did Gideon's son Abimelech desire for himself?

Abimelech desired to be the people's ruler/king. The Israelites had offered kingship to Abimelech's father Gideon (8:22-23). Gideon refused in word, declaring that the Lord was king, but his subsequent actions indicate that he assumed the position anyway, at least to some extent. He took a harem, instituted a system of worship in his hometown, and named a son "Abimelech," which means "my father is king."

15 Compare Gideon's declaration about the Lord in Judges 8:23 with the Israelites' attitude toward the Lord in the period of the Judges. See Judges 1-2 and review your answers to questions 2-3 if necessary. Read Revelation 19:16. Specifically, what will you change or do differently today in acknowledgment of Jesus' rightful lordship?

[Personal sharing]

Lesson 5 Answers

Day 1 - *Refer to Judges 10-12.*

1. According to Judges 10:6-16, how does the Lord feel about the sin of His people and about their resulting misery?

The Lord became angry because of Israel's idolatry and sold them into the hands of their enemies (10:7). However, after they repented and got rid of their idols, God "could bear Israel's misery no longer" (10:16).

2. Read Judges 11:1, 28-40. Keep in mind Israel's pagan attitudes in Jephthah's day. What adjectives would you use to describe his vow? If you are familiar with the Law of Moses, can you recall anything that should have influenced Jephthah's thinking about making that kind of vow? Was his vow even necessary?

Jephthah's vow may have demonstrated zeal, but it also indicates that he was attempting to negotiate with or even manipulate the Lord. Furthermore, the vow was rash and unnecessary. Other Judges successfully delivered Israel without making vows. The keeping of it reflected Jephthah's pagan mindset. Human sacrifice was an accepted practice among some pagans, but Jephthah should have known that the Law of Moses forbade it (Leviticus 18:21; Deuteronomy 18:10). The Law made provision for people who "belonged to the Lord" or were dedicated to Him to be redeemed by a monetary gift, not sacrificed, as were animals (Exodus 13:13, Leviticus 27:1-8). Sadly, Jephthah may have been fairly ignorant of the Law. Note: Some scholars believe the passage implies that Jephthah commuted his daughter's death sentence to a life of virginity.

3. What cultural attitudes and influences do you see creeping into private and public worship of the Lord today?

In today's Western world, there is tremendous cultural pressure for tolerance of all belief systems. Another example is the entertainment mentality, in which worshippers primarily seek emotional experiences or expect to be entertained and "spoon-fed" by speakers and musicians, instead of exercising the disciplines of Bible reading, study, and prayer. The combined effect of these two prevalent attitudes is ignorance of many important Bible doctrines. Even professing believers often have a lower, less than Biblical, view of the person and work of Jesus Christ. Their "Jesus" is a deity of their own imagination, contrived by mixing Scripture with cultural beliefs or personal ideas. A casual attitude toward sin or complete denial of it is yet another result. Many other cultural attitudes and influences may be cited.

Day 2 - *Refer to Judges 13-14.*

4. Read Judges 13:1-5, 24-25 with Numbers 6:1-8, 1 Samuel 1:10-11, 20, Luke 1:13-17, and Acts 18:18. What was the Nazirite vow and who besides Samson was a Nazirite or took a Nazirite vow?

A Nazirite vow was generally a temporary vow to set oneself apart for the Lord. The vow-maker was specifically restricted from cutting their hair, eating or drinking anything fermented or any product of the vine, and making contact with a dead body. Samuel and John the Baptist were Nazirites. Paul seems to have taken a Nazirite vow on one occasion. Reportedly, many early Christians did so.

5 From Judges 13-16, give examples of ways the Lord worked through Israel's deliverer (Judge), Samson, despite Samson's unusual and even questionable choices and methods.

> **a)** Judges 14:1-4
>
> Samson chose a pagan Philistine as his wife. Surprisingly, 14:4 says, "…this was from the Lord, who was seeking an occasion to confront the Philistines."
>
> **b)** Judges 14:10-19
>
> Samson killed 30 Philistines from Ashkelon in order to get their clothing (14:19).
>
> **c)** Judges 15:1-8
>
> When Samson's father-in-law gave his wife to his friend, Samson became angry and torched the Philistines' fields. After she and her father were murdered, Samson retaliated again, viciously slaughtering the Philistines who had burned them to death (15:8).
>
> **d)** Judges 15:11-15
>
> Samson killed 1,000 Philistines with a donkey's jawbone.
>
> **e)** Judges 16:4-31
>
> Samson killed more Philistines in his death than he had in his life. He pushed down the supports of the Philistines' temple while it was full of the people who had come to see a blind man "perform."

6 What does Samson's story teach you about whom the Lord can use to accomplish His purposes? How might this cause you to think differently about current national and international events and leaders? Give specific examples, without slandering any one particular leader or group of leaders.

Unlike the other judges, Samson functioned more as a lone commando than as a battle commander. Even though Samson's methods were very unorthodox, God worked through him to punish Israel's enemy. God can work through anyone or anything He chooses to accomplish His good purposes. [Personal sharing]

Day 3 - *Refer to Judges 17-18.*

7 What signs of spiritual chaos can you find in the following verses?

> **a)** Judges 17:3-4 (See Exodus 20:4.)
>
> Silver that had been consecrated to the Lord was used to make an idol.
>
> **b)** Judges 17:1, 5 and 10-12 (See Exodus 40:12-15 and Numbers 18:1, 7.) *Note: Although Aaron and his sons descended from the line of Levi, under the Mosaic law, only Aaron's descendants had the right to be priests, not the Levites in general.*
>
> The Israelites were not to have any idols. Furthermore, only Levites who descended from Aaron could serve as Israel's priests. Micah made idols and hired a Levite, but not an Aaronic Levite (18:30), as his personal priest. He also installed one of his own sons, an Ephraimite (17:1), as a priest.
>
> **c)** Judges 17:13
>
> Micah was so ignorant of the Law that he actually believed God would bless him for installing these men as his priests.
>
> **d)** Judges 18:1-6, 27, 30-31
>
> The entire tribe of Dan set up an idolatrous center of worship, rather than worshipping at the Lord's house in Shiloh. Moses' own grandson was too ignorant or careless of the Law to refuse to be a priest and serve an idol!

8 At first, we may find Israel's sins incomprehensible. They were God's own people! What does 1 Corinthians 10:1-13 say about this? What specific warning do you need to take from this period in Israel's history?

1 Corinthians 10 tells us that Israel's sins were recorded as an example to warn us against thinking we could never fall into sin as they did. [Personal sharing]

Day 4 - *Refer to Judges 19-21.*

9 Read Judges 19. Which verses bear a striking resemblance to Genesis 19:4-8? Since the writer of Judges almost certainly assumed his readers would be familiar with Genesis, what point about Israel's moral condition was he making?

Judges 19:22-24 bears a striking resemblance to the account that took place at Lot's doorstep on the eve of the Lord's destruction of Sodom and Gomorrah. Both were the result of extreme wickedness. Apparently, the writer of Judges placed this particular episode near the end of the book to illustrate the depths to which Israel had plummeted morally.

10 Why did the Levite gruesomely cut his dead concubine's body into twelve pieces?

It seems that he wanted to shock all twelve tribes into taking action against those who killed his concubine.

11 Judges 20 describes a very dark hour in Israel's history that resulted from the murder of the Levite's concubine (chapter 19).

a According to Judges 20:8-11, what verdict did Israel render upon the tribe of Benjamin?

Israel determined to unite (20:11) and wage war against Benjamin, giving them "what they deserved for all this vileness done in Israel" (20:10).

b Summarize the events that followed in verses 20-21, 24-29, 35-36, and 48.

After two days of fighting, in which Benjamin overran Israel, the Israelites wept before the Lord, fasted, made sacrifices, and inquired of Him. Then, they set up an ambush and, as the Lord promised, defeated the Benjamites. Finally, they went to the towns of Benjamin, killed every living thing including animals, and set the towns on fire.

12 According to Judges 21, how did Israel ensure the tribe of Benjamin was not altogether erased?

One Israelite town failed to participate in Benjamin's judgment. The Israelites put to death all males and married women from this town and gave the unmarried girls to the few remaining male Benjamites. However, there were more male Benjamites than there were brides, so the remaining men were given the opportunity to "grab" a virgin from the unsuspecting families of a different town, Shiloh. This plan enabled the men of Israel, specifically, the men of Shiloh, to keep their vow against giving their daughters to the Benjamites, while still ensuring the continuation of the tribe.

13 Read Judges 17:6 and 21:25. How does this summary of Israel's condition compare to the moral climate in your own culture? What can you personally do to keep such thinking from prevailing among believers in your area?

These verses say, "In those days Israel had no king; everyone did as he saw fit." [Personal sharing]

Day 5 - *Refer to the book of Judges.*

14 According to Judges 8:1, 12:1-4, and 20:18-48, what politically significant consequence resulted from Israel's spiritual decline?

Spiritual decline resulted in civic and tribal disunity and eventually a civil war that almost wiped out an entire tribe.

15 Read Romans 15:5-6. Are you in a relationship or group in which an absence of true spirituality is fostering disunity? If so, what can you do about it?

[Personal sharing]

Lesson 6 Answers

Day 1 - *Read Ruth 1.*

1 Which statements summarize Naomi's catastrophic state? Include the verse numbers.

Ruth 1:5 says, "Naomi was left without her two sons and her husband." In patriarchal cultures, this was a statement of catastrophic implications. In 1:13 and 10-21, Naomi indicated that the Lord's hand was against her, leaving her bitter and "empty."

2 In chapter 1, which of Ruth's words and actions indicate she had experienced a spiritual conversion?

In stating, "your people will be my people and your God my God" (1:16-17), Ruth indicated her willingness to abandon her Moabite culture, family, and gods in order to worship Yahweh and align herself with His people. She backed up her declaration with action, suggesting true Biblical, saving faith (faith working itself out in actions [James 2:14-26]).

3 Reread Ruth 1:20-21.

a) Have you ever experienced a season of emptiness right after a time of fullness? If so, briefly describe it.

[Personal sharing]

b) What are the root causes of suffering according to God's word?

Hebrews 12:5-11	The Lord's hand of discipline comes for our training. He never disciplines His children out of spite or because He has a mean streak. God's discipline is always remedial and redemptive in nature.
2 Corinthians 12:7-9a	Some suffering comes directly from the enemy, the Satanic realm. Even then, God intends to work through it for good.
Genesis 3:17-19, Romans 8:22 (the world's general condition)	We live in a fallen world.
Proverbs 1:22, Romans 6:23a, Galatians 6:7-8	Even after God forgives us, our personal sin has consequences that often remain. We reap what we sow.
Proverbs 11:29a, Acts 20:3, 1 Corinthians 16:9b	Others' sin often impacts our lives.

c) If you are presently in an empty season of life, what do Psalm 30:5b, Romans 8:28-29, 1 Corinthians 10:13, and 1 Peter 5:10 say that encourages you?

These passages encourage those who are hurting or empty that in every circumstance, God is always working toward the good of making His children Christlike. He knows the limits of how much we can bear and He will restore us in His right time.

Day 2 - *Read Ruth 2.*

4. In what verses and phrases of Ruth 2 do you see God at work behind the scenes?

According to Ruth 2:3-4, circumstances occurred that were more than coincidental, as indicated by the phrases "as it turned out" and "just then." God's providential work behind the scenes is implied.

5. What character qualities of Ruth and Boaz does chapter 2 reveal?

Ruth's willingness to work to support her mother-in-law shows her love, industriousness, and initiative (2:2). Boaz's greeting of his workers, "The Lord be with you," shows friendliness, genuine concern for others, and spiritual-mindedness (2:4). Ruth worked steadily except for a short rest, indicating that she was hard-working (2:7). Boaz provided a safe place for Ruth to work; he was a kind man (2:8). Ruth bowed down to Boaz and responded in a way that indicates humility (2:10 and 13). Boaz recounted Ruth's kindness toward her mother-in-law, reminding us that Ruth was loyal, kind, and unselfish (2:11). Boaz's blessing to Ruth implies even more clearly that he was a godly man (2:12). Boaz made provisions for Ruth, indicating that he was generous and kind (2:14-16). Ruth conformed her work habits to what Boaz and her mother-in-law recommended, proving she was submissive and teachable. Furthermore, once she arrived in Israel, she did not run off to seek a life of her own but continued living with her mother-in-law. Ruth was faithful (2:23).

6. Boaz was a blessing to Ruth and Ruth was a blessing to Naomi. Who has God placed in your life that you could seek to bless? What specific steps will you take this week?

[Personal sharing]

Day 3 - *Read Ruth 3.*

7. Summarize Naomi's plan as described in Ruth 3. In what ways would this plan have been risky for Ruth?

Naomi told Ruth to go to the threshing floor at night, cleanly washed, dressed, and perfumed. Once Boaz retired for the night, she was to remove the covering from his feet and lie down. This plan required Ruth to travel alone in the dark which was unsafe for a woman, hide until Boaz retired while hoping not to be discovered, slip into his presence without anyone else noticing, and make a silent request of him by lying by his uncovered feet. Boaz could have outright rejected her or even had her punished.

8. What was Boaz's response to Ruth's initiative?

Boaz called Ruth's initiative and interest in him a kindness since he was no longer a young man. He assured her that he would take the necessary steps to become her kinsman-redeemer. First, he had to offer the opportunity and responsibility to a closer relative. Boaz instructed Ruth to remain in the safety of his presence until daylight, and then loaded her with food for her mother-in-law.

9. What "faith-risk" is God asking you to take right now?

[Personal sharing]

Day 4 - *Read Ruth 4.*

10 Reread Ruth 2:20, 3:9, 12-13, and 4:1. What insights do you gain into the nature of the "kinsman-redeemer" role from Ruth 4?

Both Boaz and another man (a nearer "kin") are called "kinsman-redeemers." 3:13 implies that either of these two men could "redeem" Ruth. In chapter 4, we learn that the kinsman-redeemer was required to redeem Naomi's land. Additionally, the one who bought the land acquired the dead man's widow as his wife--in this case, Ruth, not Naomi, probably since Naomi was past child-bearing years, in order to maintain the lineage of the dead man whose property was purchased. The Mosaic Law did not link redemption of property with levirate marriage, but Ruth 4 indicates that doing so had become customary. The chapter hints that taking this role could put a man's personal estate at risk. Finally, the elders of the town blessed Boaz for his willingness to redeem Ruth, thereby implying that it was an act of generosity on Boaz's part. Apparently, Ruth was not the only one who took a risk.

11 Examine the genealogy in Ruth 4:16-22. According to Genesis 46:12, who was Perez's father? According to the genealogy in Ruth, what was Ruth's relationship to King David?

Judah, son of Israel, was Perez's father. Ruth was the great-grandmother of King David. The account of Ruth and Naomi's lives is the only history of King David's ancestry recorded in the Bible.

12 Re-read Ruth 4:17a in consideration of Ruth 1:21. Then, read Romans 15:13. In which personal circumstance does the "God of hope" want you to "overflow with hope by the power of the Holy Spirit"?

God gave Naomi a son, when previously she had been destitute ("empty"). God can turn around any misfortune, and even work through what seems hopeless to bring about surprising and good things. [Personal sharing]

Day 5 - *Refer to the book of Ruth.*

13 Consider the words in Ruth 4:13-17 with Ruth 1:5, 6, 13, and 21. Who is the story of Ruth really about?

The book of Ruth is actually the story of Naomi's life.

14 Reread Ruth 1:1 with Judges 21:25. Recalling what you learned from the two previous lessons on Judges, what do you find surprising about the fact that the book of Ruth is set in the period of the Judges?

The book of Judges is depressing to the point of being difficult to read and covers history in a broad way. By contrast, the book of Ruth is a very personal story of God's involvement in the life of one family. Judges shows God's involvement in national life, while Ruth shows God's involvement in personal life. Even more importantly, at a time when Israel largely had no interest in God (Judges 21:25), a Moabite, and a woman, no less, appears in the Scriptures as a model of true faith and evidence that at least one family did acknowledge Yahweh as king.

15 How does the book of Ruth show that God's plan for any one person's life has implications that extend far beyond that one life alone? Give a specific example of how this truth ought to influence your attitude toward the role(s) in life the Lord has presently given you.

In chapter one, Naomi was focused on her own personal crisis. She was so self-absorbed that she could not even see Ruth's loyalty as an evidence of God's faithfulness. The rest of the story shows that God had a plan in allowing Naomi's misfortune. Through Ruth's marriage to Boaz, the kinsman-redeemer, God, placed Ruth, and indirectly, Naomi in the Messianic line of ancestry. [Personal sharing]

Lesson 7 Answers

Day 1 - *Read 1 Samuel 1.*

1. List the similarities between Ruth/Naomi's story and Hannah's story.

Both are stories about women who lived in the time of the Judges and were childless. Both stories open with an account of a journey. Naomi and Hannah were in deep distress. As a result of divine intervention, both Ruth and Hannah gave birth to sons who were important Bible characters.

2. Research the subjects of marriage and polygamy in the following passages and record your findings.
>Genesis 2:22-25, 16:1-6, 29:26-32 with 30:1
>1 Samuel 1:1-7 and 2 Samuel 3:1-5 with 13:1-2, 14, 20, 28-29
>1 Corinthians 7:1-4 and Titus 1:6

Genesis indicates that God intended one man and one woman to become one flesh in marriage. The New Testament also portrays marriage as being between one man and one woman. These two individuals belong exclusively to God and to one another. Although the Old Testament records the cultural practice of polygamy by pagans and God's people alike, God never condoned it. In fact, almost every Biblical story involving polygamy indicates that family conflict and heartache resulted.

3. 1 Samuel 1:18 says that Hannah's "face was no longer downcast."

a) Does the passage directly indicate that she knew God would give her a child?

No, the Bible does not say exactly what lifted Hannah's countenance. Perhaps the Lord gave Hannah a confident assurance that He would give her a son, either while she was praying or after Eli the priest blessed her ("May the God of Israel grant you what you have asked of Him"). It is also possible that her outlook changed simply because her confidence in the Lord and His plan, whatever it might be, was renewed.

b) What foundational Biblical truths give perspective when we are awaiting an answer to prayer? See Deuteronomy 7:9, Psalm 106:1, Proverbs 15:29, and Romans 8:26-28, 34.

God is good, loving, faithful, hears our prayers, and will answer them according to what He knows is best. The Holy Spirit interprets our prayers to the Father, according to His will, and Jesus is at God's right hand, interceding for us.

c) With regard to which yet unanswered prayer do you need this Biblical perspective?
[Personal sharing]

Day 2 - *Refer to 1 Samuel 1.*

4. What do the following passages indicate about God's appraisal of women, compared with the view of the traditional, patriarchal, Eastern Culture?
>Judges 4:4, 9, 21, 9:53; Ruth 4:13-22; 1 Samuel 1:20; Matthew 1:1, 3, 5, 6

God's word presents a high view of women and their social influence.

5. How did Hannah intend to keep the vow she made in 1 Samuel 1:11, according to 1:22, 24-28?

Hannah vowed to give her son to the Lord all the days of his life and that no razor would ever be used on his head (1 Samuel 1:11, a Nazarite vow). According to 1:22, 24-28, Hannah brought Samuel to Eli in Shiloh to serve the Lord for his entire life.

6. What reasons did Hannah have to trust or distrust Eli with the care of her precious little Samuel? See 1 Samuel 1; 2:12, 22-23; and 3:13. How does her decision to leave Samuel impact your thinking about a struggle or decision you face?

It is possible that Hannah had great confidence in Eli, yet it seems unlikely. Eli was God's priest. He had blessed Hannah (1:17). However, Eli seems to have been a poor father. His sons had a reputation for being wicked (1 Samuel 2:22-23) and he failed to restrain them (3:13). Nevertheless, Hannah had made a vow to God that she intended to keep. Surely the God who had sustained her in childless state and miraculously opened her womb was also capable of delivering, sustaining, and mightily using Samuel. She may have had concerns about Eli, but she trusted God. [Personal sharing]

Day 3 - *Read 1 Samuel 2.*

7. Compare Hannah's prayer in 1 Samuel 2:1-10 with Mary's "song" in Luke 1:46-55. What subjects do both women address?

Rejoicing in the Lord is the common theme. Hannah addressed the subjects of deliverance from an enemy (most likely Peninnah, 2:1), the Lord's salvation (2:2), humble confidence in the Lord versus arrogant boasting (2:3), fulfillment of desires (2:5), and justice (2:3-10). Mary's song also addresses some of these subjects: humility (Luke 1:48), justice (Luke 1:51-52), and fulfillment of desires (Luke 1:51), but also speaks of God's goodness and mercy (Luke 1:49, 54-55).

8. What example of Eli's sons' disregard for the Lord is recorded in 1 Samuel 2:12-17? See Leviticus 3:16, 7:29-31.

God gave His priests the privilege of eating portions of the Israelites' sacrifices. Apparently, the general custom involved plunging a fork into the boiling meat and retaining whatever portion came up (1 Samuel 2:13-14). According to the Mosaic Law (Leviticus 3, 7), other parts of the sacrifice, including the fat, were to be burned. Eli's sons wanted the entire offering, including the fat, and took it by force. They were disobeying the Lord, disrespecting worshippers, and making a mockery of the system of sacrifices.

9. Compare 1 Samuel 2:5, 20-21 with Joel 2:25a and Romans 11:35-36. Even though God owes us nothing, can you think of a time when He graciously extended special blessing to you after a season of difficulty or suffering? If so, write out your own words of praise to Him.

[Personal sharing]

Day 4 - *Refer to 1 Samuel 2.*

10. In 1 Samuel 2:12-36, the author clearly intended to sharply contrast the characters. Describe the contrasts and include verse numbers.

The chapter clearly contrasts Eli's sons and Samuel, the wicked and the righteous. 1 Samuel 2:12-17 describes Eli's sons' wickedness in making a mockery of the Lord's sacrifices. The very next verse (2:18) describes Samuel's faithful ministry before the Lord. 2:22-25 says that Eli's sons were sleeping with the women who served at the Tabernacle and ignored their father's rebuke. The following verse (2:26) describes Samuel, who continued "to grow in stature and in favor with the Lord and with men." 2:27-34 records a prophecy that Eli's family would be dishonored and cursed. 2:35-36 contrast Eli's family line with that of a faithful priest. God would raise up a faithful priest who would do what was in God's heart and mind and whose house He would firmly establish. Some think prophecy was fulfilled in Zadok's replacement of Abiathar as priest in Solomon's day (1 Kings 2:27, 35).

11. What did the Lord accuse Eli of in 1 Samuel 2:27-36, and what consequences would he suffer?

In 2:28-29, the Lord accused Eli of taking the great privilege of high priesthood too lightly, ignoring and scorning God's prescribed use of the sacrifices by fattening themselves on what belonged to the Lord, and honoring his sons over the Lord. The Lord said that as a result, Eli's descendants would meet early deaths--Hophni and Phinehas would die on the same day--and so weaken the priestly line that they would eventually beg to simply make a living within the priesthood.

12. What promise and warning do you find in 1 Samuel 2:30, Psalm 18:25-27, and Proverbs 3:34? Name some specific ways you will plan to honor the Lord in your life this week.

The Lord promises to show honor, faithfulness and grace to those who show honor, humility, and faithfulness in their relationship with Him. However, He warns those who despise Him and are prideful and crooked that they will be treated with the same disdain, mockery, and shrewdness. [Personal sharing]

Day 5 - *Read 1 Samuel 3.*

13. Compare 1 Samuel 3:1 with Judges 21:25 and recall the spiritually dark period in which these events took place.

The days of the Judges of Israel in which Samuel lived were spiritually dark. 1 Samuel 3:1 says, "In those days the word of the Lord was rare; there were not many visions." Judges 21:25 says, "...Everyone did as they saw fit."

14. What was located in Shiloh? This was the town where Elkanah and his family traveled annually for worship, the location where Hannah left Samuel to serve the Lord, and the place where Samuel was ministering when the Lord spoke to him. See Exodus 40:1-17, Joshua 18:1, Judges 18:31, and 1 Samuel 1:3, 24, 3:21.

The Tabernacle with the Ark of the Covenant, the place where God's presence symbolically dwelt, was set up in Shiloh under Joshua's leadership during the period of Israel's conquest. They remained there until later in the life of Samuel, when it was captured by the Philistines and returned via Beth Shemesh to Kiriath Jearim (1 Samuel 6-7).

15. According to 1 Samuel 3:9-10, Samuel took Eli's advice, remained where he was lying, and said, "Speak, Lord, for your servant is listening." What might be keeping you from hearing the Lord's voice today?

Personal sharing could include busyness, conviction of unconfessed sin, unwillingness to obey the Lord's past instructions, etc.

Lesson 8 Answers

Day 1 - *Read 1 Samuel 4:1-11.*

1. After the Philistines defeated the Israelites in battle (1 Samuel 4:2), what did the Israelites conclude had gone wrong and why would they have come to this conclusion? Consider 1 Samuel 4:4 in light of God's words in Exodus 25:20-22, 29:42-46 and Israel's past experiences in Numbers 7:89, Joshua 6:6-11, 20-21.

The Israelites concluded that the Lord would give them victory if the Ark of the Covenant was present. They had carried it into battle in Joshua's day (Joshua 6). It was the place where God was symbolically present.

2. What do we know about the spiritual condition of the Israelites in the period of the Judges that offers insight about why their solution failed? Compare Judges 2:19-22, 21:25 and 1 Samuel 3:1 with Deuteronomy 6:5 and 1 Peter 4:17.

The Israelites were idolatrous during the period of the Judges. It was not a time when they typically heard from God (1 Samuel 3:1). Furthermore, because of their unfaithfulness, the Lord had told them that He would not finish driving out their enemies. He left them to test Israel's obedience. While it is possible that the Israelites brought the Ark into battle as a sign of repentance and recommitment, since the Ark did not bring victory, their hearts probably hadn't truly changed. In view of the spiritual ignorance, superstition, and idolatry that characterized the period of the Judges, Israel probably had a mistaken view of the Ark. They probably saw it as a substitute for the Lord Himself, a talisman that would bring them luck. They sought a formula instead of seeking God, a symbol of worship rather than the object of worship, and a solution to a physical battle without first considering their own spiritual battle. They thought the Ark would bring victory over their enemies. Instead, they brought judgment upon themselves.

3. Reread 1 Samuel 4:6-9. The Philistines had a confused view about the God of Israel.

(a) How was their view a reflection of what Israel had modeled to them? Cross reference 1 Samuel 4:6-8 with Exodus 20:3-6, Judges 3:5-6, 6:24-25, 8:27, 33, 10:6, and 18:30-31.

It is no surprise that, while Israel's enemies had heard what Israel's "god(s)" had done in delivering them from Egypt (Joshua 2:9-11 and 1 Samuel 4:8), they were nevertheless confused about the nature of Israel's deity. Indeed, not long after Joshua's death, the Israelites seemed confused themselves. At times, such as the battle in 1 Samuel 4, the Israelites recognized Yahweh as their God, yet as the book of Judges makes clear, they also served other gods. God had revealed Himself to Israel as the one and only true God (Exodus 20:3-7). The prevalent ancient Near Eastern view was polytheistic, with each land having one god of primary influence. Thus, the Philistines recognized Yahweh as Israel's primary deity but not as the one and only true Deity. Indeed, since the Israelites had intermarried with local peoples and adopted their polytheistic views, this had apparently become their own belief. They failed in their mission to be God's representatives to all nations (Exodus 19:6).

(b) Are you modeling anything that might leave someone confused about the God you worship? If so, what?

[Personal sharing]

Day 2 - *Read 1 Samuel 4:12-5:12.*

4. Recall and record the significance of the deaths of Hophni and Phinehas. See 1 Samuel 1-3.
Eli's two sons, Hophni and Phinehas, were wicked priests. They corrupted the system of sacrifices (2:12-17), slept with the women who worked at the tent of meeting (2:22-25), and ignored their father's rebukes (2:25). Their deaths occurred on the same day in fulfillment of prophecy (1 Samuel 2:34). According to the prophecy, their deaths would be a sign that God, as He foretold, would remove Eli's family from prominence in the priesthood and that all of his descendants would die prematurely (1 Samuel 2:30-36).

5. Summarize the story in 1 Samuel 5.
After the Philistines captured the Ark of the Lord in battle, they carried it to one of their five city-states, Ashdod, and placed it in Dagon's temple. For two successive mornings, the idol was found on its face before the Ark. After a plague involving rats and tumors caused the residents of the city to become ill and die, the Philistines moved the Ark to the city-state of Gath. When its residents also broke out in tumors, they moved it to Ekron, another of their city-states, under the residents' great objection. When the plague broke out again, the Philistines insisted their leaders send the Ark back to Israel.

6. God was not only concerned about the Israelites but also the Philistines.

(a) What opportunity did He give the Philistines to learn about and embrace Him?
Chapter 5 ends with the interesting comment that the cry of the Philistines went up to heaven. They certainly had an opportunity to know Yahweh. The very Ark of God, with all of its symbolism, was among them. They also witnessed His supreme power over nature and human life in the plagues of rats and tumors and over their deities, when Dagon repeatedly fell prostrate before the Ark.

(b) What have you learned so far in *Promised Land I* that indicates God has always been concerned about people of every culture? If you have previous Bible study experience, you may include information from Genesis through Deuteronomy.
In Joshua 2, knowledge of what God had done for Israel in the past caused the Gentile prostitute Rahab to embrace Yahweh as her own God. The Philistines had heard the very same things (1 Samuel 4:8). The book of Ruth shows God's concern for a Moabites who, presumably, came to know Him through her Israelite mother-in-law Naomi. God's covenant promise to Abraham included making him a blessing to all nations. God has always been concerned with people from every race, tongue, and nation.

(c) Do you share God's passionate concern for people of all nations? How are you currently fulfilling the Great Commission in Matthew 28:19-20?
[Personal sharing]

Day 3 - *Read 1 Samuel 6.*

7. What experiment did the Philistines conduct? Which verse summarizes it?
1 Samuel 6:9 says the Philistines decided to find out whether the plague had been brought on them by Israel's God for taking His Ark into their land or whether it occurred by chance. They put the Ark on a cattle-drawn cart, believing that if the cattle returned the Ark to Israel, the God of Israel had been angry and was responsible for the outbreak.

8. 1 Samuel 6:19 tells us the Lord put to death 70 Israelites who looked into the Ark. What had they done wrong? See Numbers 4:5, 15, 20, Joshua 3:3, 1 Samuel 6:15, 2 Samuel 6:6-7, and 1 Samuel 6:20.
According to the Law of Moses, only Levites could handle the Ark, and not even they could touch it directly or look into it. Touching and looking into the Ark was a direct violation of God's Law. The 70 residents of Beth Shemesh showed no respect for God's holiness.

9 The Israelites at Beth Shemesh asked, "Who can stand in the presence of the Lord, this holy God?" (1 Samuel 6:20).

a How did the Philistines attempt to meet God's holy standard in their own way (chapter 6)?

The Philistines offered a guilt offering to the Lord (1 Samuel 6:3) consisting of five gold tumors and five gold rats (6:4), representing the tumors and rats that were destroying their country. They were five in number to represent the five Philistine city-states and their five rulers. Their "offering" was a syncretistic blend of truth from the Torah, the need for a guilt offering, and pagan superstition of offering created images rather than a blood sacrifice. They offered rats, a detestable animal according to God's Law [Leviticus 11:29], and tumors, unclean by the Law's standard. God dealt with the Philistines more mercifully than the Israelites of Beth Shemesh who looked into the Ark (6:19).

b How do people today respond to the idea that God has a holy standard?

People today often view God's self-revelation through pagan lenses, just as the Philistines had, and attempt to appease Him by pagan methods. Like many false religions, some "Christian" churches teach salvation by works. Non-religious people respond to God's holy standard with incredulousness, irritability, or even outright anger.

c According to Hebrews 11:6 and 10:19-22, what is the sole basis upon which one can approach and appease a Holy God?

Faith in the blood of Jesus is the only basis for approaching God and the only means by which His wrath over sin is appeased.

d Which of your neighbors, co-workers, relatives, friends, or acquaintances is actively attempting to meet God's holy standard in their own way and needs to hear this good news?

[Personal sharing]

Day 4 - *Read 1 Samuel 7.*

10 Under Samuel's direction, what did the Israelites do to show they were serious about recommitting themselves to the Lord?

Samuel told Israel to rid themselves of idols (7:3-4) and then assemble for worship, fasting, and confession of sin (7:5-6).

11 Contrast the manner in which the Israelites fought the Philistines under *Hophni and Phinehas'* leadership (1 Samuel 4) versus under *Samuel's* leadership (1 Samuel 7). Include the results of both.

Under Hophni and Phinehas' leadership, the Israelites thought that relocating the Ark of the Covenant would bring them victory over the Philistines. Instead, the Philistines routed them and the Israelites lost the Ark. Samuel led Israel to victory by bringing the people back to the Lord. He had them rid themselves of idols and assemble to fast and confess sin. Samuel made a sacrifice in accordance with the Law of Moses and interceded for Israel. After this, the Lord fought for them and they were victorious over the Philistines.

12 Ebenezer means "stone of help." What do you need the Lord your Rock to help you with today? See 1 Samuel 2:2, Psalm 31:3, 46:1, 118:7, and 146:5.

[Personal sharing]

Day 5 - *Read 1 Samuel 4-7.*

13 What do each of the chapters in this lesson reveal about the power of God?

1 Samuel 4 shows the power of God in the fulfillment of prophecy through the premature deaths within Eli's family (2:32-34; 3:12; 4:11, 18, 20) and that God's power cannot be manipulated as the Israelites attempted to do with the Ark. 1 Samuel 5 shows the Lord's power in judgment on the Philistines' god, proof that He is as powerful on foreign soil as in Israel. He is Lord of all the earth and the Almighty Judge of all the earth. 1 Samuel 6 shows the Lord's power in overruling nature so that the cows carried the Ark back into Israelite territory and in judgment on the residents of Beth Shemesh. In 1 Samuel 7, the Lord "thundered" from the heavens and delivered the Israelites, also a fulfillment of prophecy (2:10).

14 List the ways in which chapter 7 indicates a reversal of the events in 1 Samuel 4-6.

The battles with the Philistines in chapters 4 and 7 occurred at locations referred to as "Ebenezer." Either these were two different locations with the same name or in chapters 4-5 the writer used the name anachronistically to identify it as the same place so named by Samuel in chapter 7. A place of Israel's former defeat became a place of victory. Secondly, Samuel's godly leadership (bringing the Israelites together in prayer and repentance) contrasts with the wicked leadership of Eli's sons, who took advantage of the people and the priesthood and misused the Ark. Thirdly, the Israelites previously sought a formula for victory and ignored their sin. In chapter 7, they turned to the Lord with all their hearts. Fourthly, instead of fighting against Israel, as the Lord had at Beth Shemesh (6:19), in chapter 7, He fought for them. Finally, in chapter 7, the towns the Philistines had previously taken from Israel were returned and the two lands stopped fighting.

15 Israel experienced reversals of former misfortunes under Samuel's godly leadership as a result of their sincere repentance. What kinds of reversals have occurred in your life since you first repented of your sins? What specific change or reversal will you ask the Almighty God to begin making within you today? See Philippians 2:12-13.

[Personal sharing]

Lesson 9 Answers

Day 1 - *Read 1 Samuel 8.*

1 List the reasons Israel wanted Samuel to appoint a king over them and include verse numbers.
Israel wanted a king because Samuel had no qualified successor (8:1-5). They wanted to have a government more like that of their neighbors (8:5). The system of Judges did not normally pass from father to son, whereas a monarchy would provide a succession of leaders. They wanted a king to lead them in their battles (8:20). Most significantly, Israel wanted a king because they had rejected the Lord's theocratic rule (8:7).

2 According to God's warning, how would Israel's kings negatively impact the people?
Under their kings, the Israelites' sons would serve the king by running in front of his chariots (8:11) and as military leaders, farmers, and makers of weapons and equipment (8:12). Their daughters would be his perfumers, cooks, and bakers (8:13). The king would take the best of the Israelites' fields, vineyards, groves, and a tenth of their produce (8:14-15). Their servants and animals would also be taken for the king's use so that a tenth of their flocks would belong to him, and they themselves would become his slaves (8:16-17). The Israelites would cry out for relief from the king's oppression, but the Lord would not answer them in that day (8:18).

3 Reread 1 Samuel 8:6-8. Samuel experienced a sense of rejection, but ultimately, it was God Himself the Israelites were rejecting. Read John 15:20 and 2 Corinthians 2:14-16. How do these passages challenge or comfort you? Be as specific as possible to your own personal circumstances.
[Personal sharing]

Day 2 - *Read 1 Samuel 9.*

4 Record all you learn about Saul, his family, Samuel, and Samuel's duties from 1 Samuel 9.
Saul's father Kish was a Benjamite of standing (9:1). Saul was "impressive...without equal...a head taller than [the other Israelites]" (9:2). His father was a farmer who owned donkeys and servants (9:3). Saul did not seem to have ever met Samuel personally before this (9:18). Finally, Saul is depicted as spiritually obtuse. Samuel was highly respected (9:6) and known as a "seer," the old name for a prophet (9:9). Because he was a prophet, he was sometimes asked to help ascertain personal information, such as the location of lost animals (9:6, 20). He was able to reveal all that was in a man's heart (9:19) and everything he said came true because he was a true prophet of God (9:6, also 3:19). As a Levitical priest (1 Chronicles 6:26), he blessed sacrifices (9:13). Samuel had authority among the people (9:22-24) and is depicted as spiritually mature and patient, awaiting and responding to God's instructions.

5 Read Deuteronomy 18:21-22 with 1 Samuel 3:19 and 9:6. What proved that a person was a true prophet of God?
A true prophet of the Lord had to have 100% accuracy in their predictions. Everything they said came to pass.

6 Reread 1 Samuel 9:14-17 with Proverbs 16:9. When Saul set out to find "the seer," he had no idea that his encounter with Samuel had been providentially arranged. Is there a person you have recently encountered, or even someone you have known a while, who might be in your life by divine orchestration? Will you ask the Lord to put a name in your mind and begin revealing His intended purpose in the intersection of your lives? Perhaps there is something He wants you to learn from this person or some way He wants to use you in their lives.
[Personal sharing]

Day 3 - *Read 1 Samuel 10.*

7. Reread 1 Samuel 8:22 as a reminder that Israel was waiting for Samuel to appoint a king. What indications does chapter 10 give that Saul was in no way positioning himself to become Israel's king and perhaps was even hesitant to take the role?

Even after Samuel anointed Saul king (10:1), Saul was inexplicably absent at his own coronation, hiding in the baggage while his identity as the new king was being revealed by the casting of lots (10:22-23). 1 Samuel 10 portrays Saul as genuinely humble at best or unwise and unwilling at worst.

8. In addition to its use for fuel, cosmetic, and medicinal purposes, the Bible also speaks of oil as being used for anointing, which meant setting apart for a special purpose. 1 Samuel 10:1 says that Samuel anointed Saul with oil.

(a) Record what you learn about anointing from the following passages:
   Exodus 30:23-33; 1 Samuel 10:1, 6 and 16:13; 2 Corinthians 1:21-22; 1 John 2:20, 27.

An aromatic blend of oil, "the work of a perfumer" (Exodus 30:25), was used to anoint the Tent of Meeting and all its furnishings, including the Ark of the Covenant. The purpose of anointing them was to "consecrate them so they would be holy and whatever touched them would be holy" (Exodus 30:29). The priests, Aaron and his sons, were also anointed with this special oil as a means of consecration for the priesthood (Exodus 30:30). Samuel poured oil from a flask on Saul's head to anoint him as the leader of God's "inheritance" (1 Samuel 10:1). Following his anointing, the Spirit of the Lord came upon Saul in power and he was changed into a different person (1 Samuel 10:6). Later, Samuel anointed David with oil and "from that day on the Spirit of the Lord came upon David in power" (1 Samuel 16:13). 2 Corinthians 1:21-22 says God has anointed believers, setting His seal of ownership on them, and putting His Spirit in their hearts as a deposit, guaranteeing what is to come. 1 John 2:20 says that believers are anointed "from the Holy One" and know the truth. 1 John 2:27 refers to the fact that a believer's anointing cannot be undone and that it "teaches you about all things." These New Testament passages clearly portray a connection between anointing and the presence of the Holy Spirit. To be anointed or consecrated is to be set apart for a unique purpose of God. "Messiah" means Anointed One.

(b) Describe your present attitude toward a particular circumstance. Then, explain how knowing that *you* have been set apart and equipped for God's special purpose can change it.

[Personal sharing]

Day 4 - *Read 1 Samuel 11.*

9. Describe the events in 1 Samuel 11 and their relationship to Saul's confirmation as king at the end of the chapter.

The Ammonites had been a threat to Israel (1 Samuel 12:12 with 11:1). The Ammonite leader, Nahash, besieged Jabesh Gilead. The elders of this Israelite town sent a messenger throughout Israel asking to be rescued. They did not directly contact Saul, an indication that Saul's leadership had not been widely accepted. The facts that one town was free to make a treaty on its own with a foreign invader (11:1) and that the people of Jabesh had no assurance that other tribes would come to their rescue (11:3) are also evidence of the lack of unity among the tribes and towns of Israel. Saul was in his field behind his oxen when the message came (11:5). "The Spirit of God came upon him in power" (11:6). He cut his oxen into pieces and sent the pieces with messengers throughout the land, a means of mustering troops (11:7-8). Following Saul's victory over the Ammonites, Samuel gathered the people in Gilgal to reaffirm the kingship (11:14). Saul's military victory seems to have been the final evidence the Israelites needed to fully rally behind him as their king.

10. According to 1 Samuel 11:7, what was behind the Israelites' motivation to unite and defend Jabesh Gilead? Was it fear of either Saul or Samuel?

Although Saul challenged the Israelites in a threatening manner, the verse says that the reason they united to defend Jabesh Gilead was because "the terror of the Lord fell on the people."

11. At this period in Israel's history, it seemed unlikely that its disconnected tribes could unite to defend one town. Is there someone you know, and need to pray for, who has a heart that seems unlikely or impossible to change?

[Personal sharing]

Day 5 - *Read 1 Samuel 12.*

12. Samuel began his farewell speech by reminding the Israelites that he had proven himself trustworthy (1 Samuel 12:1-5). After considering the remainder of his speech, explain why it was important for him to begin as he did.

Samuel accused the Israelites of rejecting the Lord in asking for a king (12:6-17). Before he confronted them with evidence (12:7), he established his credibility as their Judge.

13. Was it God's will for Israel to have a king or not? What was God's purpose with regard to kingship in Israel? Refer to Genesis 17:6 (God's promise to Abraham), Deuteronomy 17:14-20 (Moses' instructions to the Israelites just before they entered the Promised Land), and 1 Samuel 8:5-7, 10:1, 11:1 with 12:12, 14, 17, 19.

God told Abraham that kings would come from his body. He also gave instructions about kingship to the Israelites who first entered Canaan. God intended that the kings in Israel would be under his theocratic kingship. They would lead His people, under His supervision. David was a king who mostly did this well. Saul, on the other hand, did not meet this expectation at all. In 1 Samuel 10:1, Samuel reminded Saul that the people belonged to the Lord. All of these facts indicate that having a king was not, in and of itself, an evil thing. However, the Israelites' motivation and timing was wrong. As Samuel reminded them (1 Samuel 12), God had faithfully provided deliverance for them every time they repented and sought his favor. Perhaps the Israelites' demand for a king was motivated by a desire for permanent leadership, without any responsibility to maintain humble dependence on God. Samuel saw their unwillingness to depend on the Lord as rebellion and a rejection of Him. Nevertheless, the Lord allowed Israel the kingship she sought and faithfully used her kings, sometimes to bless Israel and sometimes to discipline her. God blessed the kings who understood they served under His ultimate authority and made them a blessing to the Israelites. The kings who sought personal gain and independence from God did not have His blessing and oppressed Israel.

14. Based upon what you have discovered thus far in Promised Land 1, what needs in Israel did God meet by giving them their first king?

Through Saul, the Lord met Israel's needs for military leadership and political unification.

15. Examine each phrase at the close of Samuel's speech (1 Samuel 12:20-25) and list the elements of spiritual leadership Samuel modeled. Which example will you follow or which instruction will you share with someone this week?

Samuel's exhortation was well balanced: encouragement with warning, accountability with instruction, and perspective with prayer. He gave encouragement ("Do not be afraid"), even in the context of confronting them ("You have done evil; yet do not turn away from the Lord, but serve the Lord with all your heart"). He gave clear warnings to them ("Do not turn away after useless idols;" "yet if you persist in doing evil, both you and your king will be swept away"). He honestly assessed the things they valued ("[your idols] can do you no good, nor can they rescue you, because they are useless"). Samuel pointed the Israelites to God ("for the sake of His great name the Lord will not reject His people, because the Lord was pleased to make you His own;" "be sure to fear the Lord and serve him faithfully with all your heart;" "consider what great things he has done for you"), prayed on their behalf ("far be it from me that I should sin against the Lord by failing to pray for you"), and instructed the Israelites ("and I will teach you the way that is good and right"). [Personal sharing]

Closing Summary Principles

Introduction

- We experience abundant life to the degree that we submit to God's authority over us.
- Submitting to God's authority begins with trusting His goodness.

Lesson 1

- Meditating on and applying God's word are foundational to spiritual victory.
- Victorious Christian living requires faith.
- A victorious life is the result of daily living out the Gospel.

Lesson 2

- God's instructions sometimes contradict human logic.
- Constant alertness to dangers prevents us from being lulled into a false sense of security and a resulting attitude of self-reliance.
- "The Lord has not given us a spirit of timidity" (2 Timothy 1:7).

Lesson 3

- Promised Land dwellers experience the thrill of discovering that the indwelling Holy Spirit is the Spirit of Power.
- Promised Land dwellers experience the joy of discovering that God Himself is their inheritance.
- Promised Land dwellers experience the blessing of discovering they have a spiritual family.

Lesson 4

- We worship what we value the most.
- Small sins lead to big problems.

Lesson 5

- Bargaining with God is unnecessary and can end in disappointment.
- Living according to our passions is perilous.
- As goes the home, so goes the nation.

Lesson 6

- Viewing our circumstances with spiritual eyes renews our perspective.
- When we demonstrate "hesed" to hurting people, they are sometimes awakened to God's providential involvement in their lives.
- God's plan for each believer's life extends far beyond the impact to him or her alone.

Principles Cont.

Lesson 7

- True prayer is transformational.
- When combined, study and meditation ingrain new habits of thinking and behavior.
- Inward solitude and silence enable us to see and hear.

Lesson 8

- Our religious acts or relics cannot manipulate God's power.
- To accept God's omnipotence is to accept our own limitations.
- Those who humble themselves before the Lord see His power at work on their behalf.

Lesson 9

- We should exercise caution in what we ask of the Lord, because He may give us exactly what we request.
- God's prescription for leadership requires humble dependence on Him.
- Sin breeds insecurity, but repentance and meditation on the Lord's mighty works assure us that in Him, we are secure.

Lesson 10

- God is faithful to all His promises.
- God is faithful to His people, even when they are not faithful to Him.

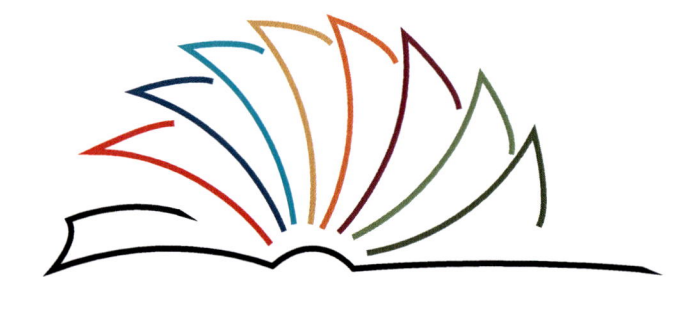

Continue the Study

NEXT UP:
PROMISED LAND II

This 15-week study presents an overview of a large portion of the Old Testament in which the Israelites repeatedly ignored the prophets' warnings and as a result, went from the height of prosperity into exile. Eventually, a small remnant returned to rebuild Jerusalem and await the promised Messiah.

Learn more about Promised Land II at
www.GODoftheWORD.org

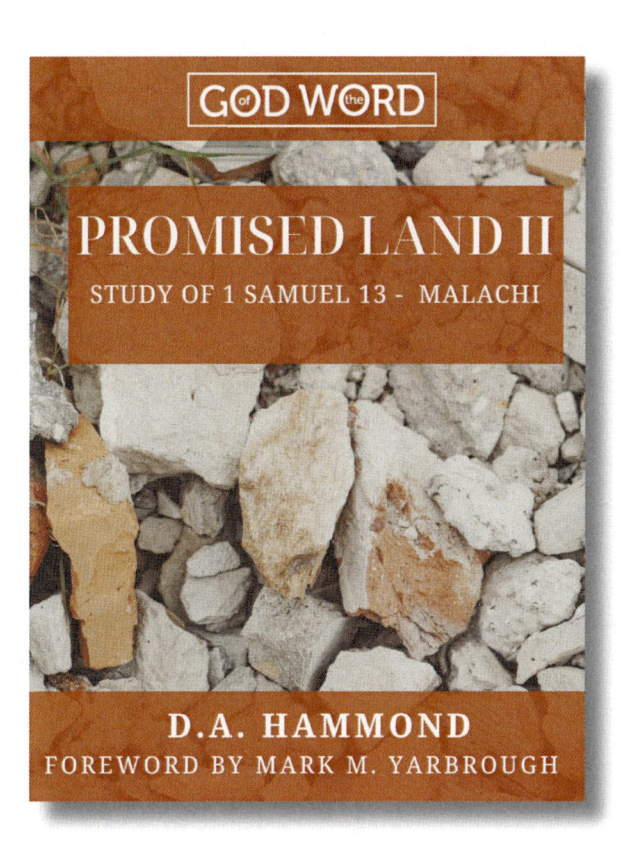

More from GOD of the WORD

▶ BEGINNINGS: Genesis 1-11

▶ PATRIARCHS: Genesis 12-50

▶ EXODUS: Exodus - Deuteronomy

▶ GOSPELS: Matthew - John

▶ ACTS I: Acts - Galatians, 1 & 2 Thessalonians, and James

▶ ACTS II: Acts, Ephesians - Colossians, and 1 Timothy - Revelation

Made in United States
Orlando, FL
01 February 2025